himself and begs forgiveness for the device that he had adopted in order to cure his friend's passion. Franceschina is condemned to "the whip and jail;" and all ends happily.

The play is enlivened by an underplot, which deals with the various tricks played by a clever knave called Cocledemoy on a vintner of Cheap, Master Mulligrub.

PROLOGUE

Slight hasty labours in this easy play
Present not what you would, but what we may:
For this vouchsafe to know,—the only end
Of our now study is, not to offend.
Yet think not but, like others, rail we could
(Best art presents not what it can but should);
And if our pen in this seem over-slight,
We strive not to instruct, but to delight.
As for some few, we know of purpose here
To tax and scout, know firm art cannot fear
Vain rage; only the highest grace we pray
Is, you'll not tax until you judge our play.
Think, and then speak: 'tis rashness, and not wit,
To speak what is in passion, and not judgment fit.
Sit then with fair expectance, and survey
Nothing but passionate man in his slight play,
Who hath this only ill, to some deem'd worst—
A modest diffidence, and self-mistrust.

Fabulæ Argumentum.

The difference betwixt the love of a courtezan and a wife is the full scope of the play, which, intermixed with the deceits of a witty city jester, fills up the comedy.

DRAMATIS PERSONÆ

Sir Lionel Freevill, and
Sir Hubert Subboys, two old knights
Young Freevill, Sir Lionel's son
Malheureux, Young Freevill's unhappy friend
Tysefew, a blunt gallant
Caqueteur, a prattling gull
Cocledemoy, a knavishly witty City Companion
Master Mulligrub, a vintner
Master Burnish, a goldsmith
Lionel, his man
Holifernes Reinscure, a barbers boy
Beatrice, and

Crispinella, Sir Hubert's daughters
Putifer, their nurse
Mistress Mulligrub
Franceschina, a Dutch Courtezan
Mary Faugh, an old woman
Three Watchmen; Pages; Officers

SCENE:—London.

THE DUTCH COURTEZAN

ACT I

SCENE I

A Street.

Enter three Pages, with lights. **MULLIGRUB, FREEVILL, MALHEUREUX, TYSEFEW,** *and* **CAQUETEUR.**

FREEVILL
Nay, comfort, my good host Shark; my good Mulligrub.

MALHEUREUX
Advance thy snout; do not suffer thy sorrowful nose to drop on thy Spanish leather jerkin, most hardly-honest Mulligrub.

FREEVILL
What, cogging Cocledemoy is run away with a neast of goblets? True, what then? they will be hammered out well enough, I warrant you.

MULLIGRUB
Sure, some wise man would find them out presently.

FREEVILL
Yes, sure, if we could find out some wise man presently.

MALHEUREUX
How was the plate lost? how did it vanish?

FREEVILL
In most sincere prose, thus: that man of much money, some wit, but less honesty, cogging Cocledemoy, comes this night late into mine hostess Mulligrub's tavern here; calls for a room; the house being full, Cocledemoy consorted with his movable chattel, his instrument of fornication, the bawd Mrs. Mary Faugh, are imparlour'd next the street; good poultry was their food, blackbird, lark, woodcock; and mine

The Dutch Courtezan by John Marston

As it was playd in the Blacke-Friars, by the Children of her Maiesties Reuels

John Marston was born to John and Maria Marston née Guarsi, and baptised on October 7th, 1576 at Wardington, Oxfordshire.

Marston entered Brasenose College, Oxford in 1592 and earned his BA in 1594. By 1595, he was in London, living in the Middle Temple. His interests were in poetry and play writing, although his father's will of 1599 hopes that he would not further pursue such vanities.

His brief career in literature began with the fashionable genres of erotic epyllion and satire; erotic plays for boy actors to be performed before educated young men and members of the inns of court.

In 1598, he published 'The Metamorphosis of Pigmalion's Image and Certaine Satyres', a book of poetry. He also published 'The Scourge of Villanie', in 1598.

'Histriomastix' regarded as his first play was produced 1599. It's performance kicked off an episode in literary history known as the War of the Theatres; a literary feud between Marston, Jonson and Dekker that lasted until 1602.

However, the playwrights were later reconciled; Marston wrote a prefatory poem for Jonson's 'Sejanus' in 1605 and dedicated 'The Malcontent' to him.

Beyond this episode Marston's career continued to gather both strength, assets and followers. In 1603, he became a shareholder in the Children of Blackfriars company. He wrote and produced two plays with the company. The first was 'The Malcontent' in 1603, his most famous play. His second was 'The Dutch Courtesan', a satire on lust and hypocrisy, in 1604-5.

In 1605, he worked with George Chapman and Ben Jonson on 'Eastward Ho', a satire of popular taste and the vain imaginings of wealth to be found in the colony of Virginia.

Marston took the theatre world by surprise when he gave up writing plays in 1609 at the age of thirty-three. He sold his shares in the company of Blackfriars. His departure from the literary scene may have been because of further offence he gave to the king. The king suspended performances at Blackfriars and had Marston imprisoned.

On 24th September 1609 he was made a deacon and them a priest on 24th December 1609. In October 1616, Marston was assigned the living of Christchurch, Hampshire.

He died (accounts vary) on either the 24th or 25th June 1634 in London and was buried in the Middle Temple Church.

Index of Contents

STORY OF THE PLAY

Young Freevill, being about to marry Beatrice, daughter to Sir Hubert Subboys, determines to break his connection with Franceschina, the Dutch Courtezan. He introduces to Franceschina his friend Malheureux. This gentleman, who had hitherto led a strict life, is violently inflamed with passion at first sight of Franceschina. She promises to gratify his passion on one condition,—that he kills Freevill. As proof that the deed has been accomplished, he is to bring her a ring that had been presented to Freevill by Beatrice. Malheureux discloses the plot to Freevill, who undertakes to help him out of his difficulty. At a masque given in honour of the approaching marriage, Malheureux pretends to pick a quarrel with Freevill, and retires with him as though to fight a duel. Freevill is to lie hid at the house of a jeweller, while Malheureux posts with the ring to Franceschina. She hastens to communicate the news to Freevill's father and Beatrice, Freevill accompanying her in the disguise of a pander. Thereupon old Freevill and Sir Hubert Subboys, attended by officers, proceed to Franceschina's lodging, conceal themselves behind the curtain, and await the arrival of Malheureux, who comes at the hour appointed by Franceschina. They hear from his own lips a confession of the murder, arrest him, and lead him away to prison. Malheureux protests his innocence, but, as Freevill has not been near the jeweller's house, his protestations are disregarded and the day for his execution is fixed. At the last moment Freevill presents host here comes in, cries "God bless you!" and departs. A blind harper enters, craves audience, uncaseth, plays; the drawer, for female privateness' sake, is nodded out, who knowing that whosoever will hit the mark of profit must, like those that shoot in stone-bows, wink with one eye, grows blind o' the right side, and departs.

CAQUETEUR
He shall answer for that winking with one eye at the last day.

MALHEUREUX
Let him have day till then, and he will wink with both his eyes.

FREEVILL
Cocledemoy, perceiving none in the room but the blind harper (whose eyes Heaven had shut up from beholding wickedness), unclasps a casement to the street very patiently, pockets up three bowls unnaturally, thrusts his wench forth the window, and himself most preposterously, with his heels forward, follows: the unseeing harper plays on, bids the empty dishes and the treacherous candles much good do them. The drawer returns, but, out alas! not only the birds, but also the neast of goblets, were flown away. Laments are raised—

TYSEFEW
Which did not pierce the heavens.

FREEVILL
The drawers moan, mine host doth cry, the bowls are gone.

MULLIGRUB
Hic finis Priami!

MALHEUREUX
Nay, be not jaw-fall'n, my most sharking Mulligrub.

FREEVILL
'Tis your just affliction; remember the sins of the cellar, and repent, repent!

MULLIGRUB
I am not jaw-fall'n, but I will hang the coney-catching Cocledemoy; and there's an end of't.

[Exit.

CAQUETEUR
Is it a right stone? it shows well by candle-light.

FREEVILL
So do many things that are counterfeit, but I assure you this is a right diamond.

CAQUETEUR
Might I borrow it of you? it will not a little grace my finger in visitation of my mistress.

FREEVILL
Why, use it, most sweet Caqueteur, use it.

CAQUETEUR
Thanks, good sir; 'tis grown high night: gentles, rest to you.

[Exit.

TYSEFEW
A torch! Sound wench, soft sleep, and sanguine dreams to you both. On, boy!

FREEVILL
Let me bid you good rest.

MALHEUREUX
Not so, trust me, I must bring my friend home: I dare not give you up to your own company; I fear the warmth of wine and youth will draw you to some common house of lascivious entertainment.

FREEVILL
Most necessary buildings, Malheureux; ever since my intention of marriage, I do pray for their continuance.

MALHEUREUX
Loved sir, your reason?

FREEVILL
Marry, lest my house should be made one. I would have married men love the stews as Englishmen loved the Low Countries: wish war should be maintain'd there, lest it should come home to their own doors. What, not suffer a man to have a hole to put his head in, though he go to the pillory for it! Youth and appetite are above the club of Hercules.

MALHEUREUX
This lust is a most deadly sin, sure.

FREEVILL
Nay, 'tis a most lively sin, sure.

MALHEUREUX
Well, I am sure, 'tis one of the head sins.

FREEVILL
Nay, I am sure it is one of the middle sins.

MALHEUREUX
Pity 'tis grown a most daily vice.

FREEVILL
But a more nightly vice, I assure you.

MALHEUREUX

Well, 'tis a sin.

FREEVILL

Ay, or else few men would wish to go to heaven: and, not to disguise with my friend, I am now going the way of all flesh.

MALHEUREUX

Not to a courtezan?

FREEVILL

A courteous one.

MALHEUREUX

What, to a sinner?

FREEVILL

A very publican.

MALHEUREUX

Dear, my loved friend, let me be full with you:
Know, sir, the strongest argument that speaks
Against the soul's eternity is lust,
That wise man's folly, and the fool's wisdom:
But to grow wild in loose lasciviousness,
Given up to heat and sensual appetite,
Nay, to expose your health and strength and name,
Your precious time, and with that time the hope
Of due preferment, advantageous means,
Of any worthy end, to the stale use,
The common bosom of a money creature,
One that sells human flesh—a mangonist!

FREEVILL

Alas, good creatures! what would you have them do? Would you have them get their living by the curse of man, the sweat of their brows? So they do: every man must follow his trade, and every woman her occupation. A poor decayed mechanical man's wife, her husband is laid up, may not she lawfully be laid down, when her husband's only rising is by his wife's falling? A captain's wife wants means; her commander lies in open fields abroad, may not she lie in civil arms at home? A waiting gentlewoman, that had wont to take say to her lady, miscarries or so; the court misfortune throws her down; may not the city courtesy take her up? Do you know no alderman would pity such a woman's case? Why, is charity grown a sin, or relieving the poor and impotent an offence? You will say beasts take no money for their fleshly entertainment: true, because they are beasts, therefore beastly; only men give to loose, because they are men, therefore manly: and indeed, wherein should they bestow their money better? In land, the title may be crack'd; in houses, they may be burnt; in apparel, 'twill wear; in wine, alas for our pity! our throat is but short: but employ your money upon women, and a thousand to nothing, some one of them will bestow that on you which shall stick by you as long as you live; they are no ungrateful

persons, they will give quid for quo: do ye protest, they'll swear; do you rise, they'll fall; do you fall, they'll rise; do you give them the French crown, they'll give you the French—O justus justa justum! They sell their bodies: do not better persons sell their souls? nay, since all things have been sold, honour, justice, faith, nay, even God Himself,
Aye me, what base ignobleness is it
To sell the pleasure of a wanton bed!
Why do men scrape, why heap to full heaps join?
But for his mistress, who would care for coin?
For this I hold to be denied of no man,
All things are made for man, and man for woman.
Give me my fee.

MALHEUREUX
Of ill you merit well. My heart's good friend,
Leave yet at length, at length; for know this ever,
'Tis no such sin to err, but to persever.

FREEVILL
Beauty is woman's virtue, love the life's music, and woman the dainties, or second course of heaven's curious workmanship. Since then beauty, love, and woman are good, how can the love of woman's beauty be bad? and, Bonum, quo communius, eo melius: wilt then go with me?

MALHEUREUX
Whither?

FREEVILL
To a house of salvation.

MALHEUREUX
Salvation?

FREEVILL
Yes, 'twill make thee repent. Wilt go to the family of love? I will show thee my creature; a pretty nimble-ey'd Dutch tanakin; an honest soft-hearted impropriation; a soft, plump, round-cheek'd froe, that has beauty enough for her virtue, virtue enough for a woman, and woman enough for any reasonable man in my knowledge. Wilt pass along with me?

MALHEUREUX
What, to a brothel?—to behold an impudent prostitution; fie on't, I shall hate the whole sex to see her. The most odious spectacle the earth can present is an immodest vulgar woman.

FREEVILL
Good still; my brain shall keep't. You must go as you love me.

MALHEUREUX
Well, I'll go to make her loath the shame she's in; The sight of vice augments the hate of sin.

FREEVILL

The sight of vice augments the hate of sin! Very fine, perdy!

[Exeunt.

SCENE II

A Brothel.

Enter **COCLEDEMOY** and **MARY FAUGH**.

COCLEDEMOY
Mary, Mary Faugh.

MARY FAUGH
m.

COCLEDEMOY
Come, my worshipful rotten rough-bellied bawd! ha! my blue-tooth'd patroness of natural wickedness, give me the goblets.

MARY FAUGH
By yea and by nay, Master Cocledemoy, I fear you'll play the knave, and restore them.

COCLEDEMOY
No, by the lord, aunt, restitution is catholic, and thou know'st we love—

MARY FAUGH
What?

COCLEDEMOY
Oracles are ceased: tempus præteritum, doest hear, my worshipful glysterpipe, thou ungodly fire that burnt Diana's temple?—doest hear, bawd?

MARY FAUGH
In very good truthness, you are the foulest-mouth'd, profane, railing brother, call a woman the most ungodly names: I must confess, we all eat of the forbidden fruit, and for mine own part, though I am one of the family of love, and, as they say, a bawd that covers the multitude of sins, yet I trust I am none of the wicked that eat fish o' Fridays.

COCLEDEMOY
Hang toasts! I rail at thee, my worshipful organ-bellows that fills the pipes, my fine rattling fleamy cough o' the lungs, and cold with a pox? I rail at thee? what, my right precious pandress, supportress of barber-surgeons, and enhanceress of lotium and diet-drink? I rail at thee, necessary damnation? I'll make an oration, I, in praise of thy most courtly in-fashion and most pleasureable function, I.

MARY FAUGH

Ay, prithee do, I love to hear myself praised, as well as any old lady, I.

COCLEDEMOY
List then:—a bawd; first for her profession or vocation, it is most worshipful of all the twelve companies; for, as that trade is most honourable that sells the best commodities—as the draper is more worshipful than the pointmaker, the silkman more worshipful than the draper, and the goldsmith more honourable than both, little Mary, so the bawd above all: her shop has the best ware; for where these sell but cloth, satins, and jewels, she sells divine virtues, as virginity, modesty, and such rare gems; and those not like a petty chapman, by retail, but like a great merchant, by wholesale; wa, ha, ho! And who are her customers? Not base corn-cutters or sowgelders, but most rare wealthy knights, and most rare bountiful lords, are her customers. Again, whereas no trade or vocation profiteth but by the loss and displeasure of another—as the merchant thrives not but by the licentiousness of giddy and unsettled youth; the lawyer, but by the vexation of his client; the physician, but by the maladies of his patient—only my smooth-gumm'd bawd lives by others' pleasure, and only grows rich by others' rising. O merciful gain, O righteous in-come! So much for her vocation, trade, and life. As for their death, how can it be bad, since their wickedness is always before their eyes, and a death's head most commonly on their middle-finger? To conclude, 'tis most certain they must needs both live well and die well, since most commonly they live in Clerkenwell, and die in Bride-well. Dixi, Mary.

[Enter **FREEVILL** and **MALHEUREUX**.

FREEVILL
Come along, yonder's the preface or exordium to my wench, the bawd. Fetch, fetch! What! Mr. Cocledemoy, is your knaveship yet stirring? Look to it, Mulligrub lies for you.

[Enter **COCLEDEMOY**.

COCLEDEMOY
The more fool he; I can lie for myself, worshipful friend. Hang toasts! I vanish. Ha! my fine boy, thou art a scholar, and hast read Tully's Offices, my fine knave. Hang toasts!

FREEVILL
The vintner will toast you, and he catch you.

COCLEDEMOY
I will draw the vintner to the stoop, and when he runs low, tilt him. Ha! my fine knave, art going to thy recreation?

FREEVILL
Yes, my capricious rascal.

COCLEDEMOY
Thou wilt look like a fool then, by and by.

FREEVILL
Look like a fool, why?

COCLEDEMOY

Why, according to the old saying: a beggar when he is lousing of himself, looks like a philosopher; a hard-bound philosopher, when he is on the stool, looks like a tyrant; and a wise man, when he is in his belly act, looks like a fool. God give your worship good rest! grace and mercy keep your syringe straight, and your lotium unspilt.

[Enter **FRANCESCHINA**.

FREEVILL
See, sir, this is she.

MALHEUREUX
This?

FREEVILL
This.

MALHEUREUX
A courtezan?—Now, cold blood defend me! What a propension afflicts me!
O, mine aderliver love, vat sall me do to requit dis your mush affection?

FREEVILL
Marry, salute my friend, clip his neck, and kiss him welcome.
A' mine art, sir, you bin very velcome.

FREEVILL
Kiss her, man, with a more familiar affection, so. Come, what entertainment? go to your lute.

[Exit **FRANCESCHINA**.

And how dost approve my sometimes elected? She's none of your ramping cannibals that devour man's flesh, nor any of your Curtian gulfs that will never be satisfied until the best thing a man has be thrown into them. I loved her with my heart, until my soul showed me the imperfection of my body, and placed my affection on a lawful love, my modest Beatrice, which if this shortheels knew, there were no being for me with eyes before her face. But, faith, dost thou not somewhat excuse my sometimes incontinency, with her enforcive beauties? Speak.

MALHEUREUX
Hah! she is a whore, is she not?

FREEVILL
Whore? fie, whore! you may call her a courtezan, a cockatrice, or (as that worthy spirit of an eternal happiness said) a suppository. But whore! fie, 'tis not in fashion to call things by their right names. Is a great merchant a cuckold, you must say he is one of the livery. Is a great lord a fool, you must say he is weak. Is a gallant pocky, you must say he has the court scab. Come, she's your mistress or so.

[Enter **FRANCESCHINA**, with her lute.

Come, siren, your voice.

FRANCESCHINA
Vill not you stay in mine bosom to-night, love?

FREEVILL
By no means, sweet breast; this gentleman has vow'd to see me chastely laid.

FRANCESCHINA
He shall have a bed too, if dat it please him.

FREEVILL
Peace, you tender him offence; he is one of a professed abstinence. Siren, your voice and away.

[She sings to her Lute.

[THE SONG.
The dark is my delight,
So 'tis the nightingale's;
My music's in the night,
So is the nightingale's;
My body is but little,
So is the nightingale's;
I love to sleep 'gainst prickle,
So doth the nightingale.
Thanks; buss; so. The night grows old; good rest.

FRANCESCHINA
Rest to mine dear love; rest, and no long absence.

FREEVILL
Believe me, not long.

FRANCESCHINA
Sall ick not believe you long?

[Exit **FRANCESCHINA**.

FREEVILL
O yes, come, via!—away, boy—on!

[Exit, his **PAGE** lighting him.

[Re-enter **FREEVILL**, and seems to overhear **MALHEUREUX**.

MALHEUREUX
Is she unchaste—can such a one be damn'd?
O love and beauty! ye two eldest seeds
Of the vast chaos, what strong right you have

Even in things divine—our very souls!

FREEVILL [Aside]
Wha, ha, ho! come, bird, come. Stand, peace!

MALHEUREUX
Are strumpets then such things so delicate?
Can custom spoil what nature made so good?
Or is their custom bad? Beauty's for use—
I never saw a sweet face vicious!
It might be proud, inconstant, wanton, nice,
But never tainted with unnatural vice.
Their worst is, their best art is love to win—
O that to love should be or shame, or sin!

FREEVILL [Aside]
By the Lord! he's caught! Laughter eternal!

MALHEUREUX
Soul, I must love her! Destiny is weak
To my affection.—A common love!—
Blush not, faint breast!
That which is ever loved of most is best.
Let colder eld the strong'st objections move,
No love's without some lust, no life without some love.

FREEVILL
Nay, come on, good sir; what, though the most odious spectacle the world can present be an immodest vulgar woman? yet, sir, for my sake—

MALHEUREUX
Well, sir, for your sake, I'll think better of them.

FREEVILL
Do, good sir; and pardon me that have brought you in:
You know the sight of vice augments the hate of sin.

MALHEUREUX
Hah! will you go home, sir; 'tis high bedtime?

FREEVILL
With all my heart, sir; only do not chide me.
I must confess—

MALHEUREUX
A wanton lover you have been.

FREEVILL

O that to love should be or shame or sin!

MALHEUREUX
Say ye?

FREEVILL
Let colder eld the strongest objections move!

MALHEUREUX
How's this?

FREEVILL
No love's without some lust, no life without some love.

Go your ways for an apostata! I believe my cast garment must be let out in the seams for you when all is done.
Of all the fools that would all man out-thrust,

He that 'gainst Nature would seem wise is worst.

[Exeunt.

ACT II

SCENE I

Outside Sir Hubert Subboy's house, under Beatrice's window.

Enter **FREEVILL**, **PAGES** with torches and **GENTLEMEN** with music.

FREEVILL
The morn is yet but young. Here, gentlemen,
This is my Beatrice' window—this the chamber
Of my betrothèd dearest, whose chaste eyes,
Full of loved sweetness and clear cheerfulness,
Have gaged my soul to her enjoyings;
Shredding away all those weak under-branches
Of base affections and unfruitful heats.
Here bestow your music to my voice.

[A song.

[Enter **BEATRICE** above.

Always a virtuous name to my chaste love!

BEATRICE

Loved sir,
The honour of your wish return to you.
I cannot with a mistress' compliment,
Forcèd discourses, or nice art of wit,
Give entertain to your dear-wishèd presence:
But safely thus,—what hearty gratefulness,
Unsullen silence, unaffected modesty,
And an unignorant shamefastness can express,
Receive as your protested due. 'Faith, my heart,
I am your servant.
O let not my secure simplicity
Breed your mislike, as one quite void of skill;
'Tis grace enough in us not to be ill.
I can some good, and, faith, I mean no hurt;
Do not then, sweet, wrong sober ignorance.
I judge you all of virtue, and our vows
Should kill all fears that base distrust can move.
My soul, what say you—still you love?

FREEVILL

Still!
My vow is up above me, and, like time,
Irrevocable: I am sworn all yours.
No beauty shall untwine our arms, no face
In my eyes can or shall seem fair;
And would to God only to me you might
Seem only fair! Let others disesteem
Your matchless graces, so might I safer seem;
Envy I covet not. Far, far be all ostent—
Vain boasts of beauties, soft joys, and the rest:
He that is wise pants on a private breast.
So could I live in desert most unknown,
Yourself to me enough were populous;
Your eyes shall be my joys, my wine that still
Shall drown my often cares; your only voice
Shall cast a slumber on my list'ning sense;
You, with soft lip, shall only ope mine eyes
And suck their lids asunder; only you
Shall make me wish to live, and not fear death,
So on your cheeks I might yield latest breath.
O he that thus may live and thus shall die,
May well be envied of a deity.

BEATRICE

Dear, my loved heart, be not so passionate;
Nothing extreme lives long.

FREEVILL
But not to be extreme—nothing in love's extreme—
My love receives no mean.

BEATRICE
I give you faith; and, prithee, since, poor soul!
I am so easy to believe thee, make it much more pity to deceive me!
Wear this slight favour in my remembrance.

[Throweth down a ring to him.

FREEVILL
Which, when I part from,
Hope, the best of life, ever part from me.

BEATRICE
I take you and your word, which may ever live your servant. See, day is quite broke up—the best of hours.

FREEVILL
Good morrow, graceful mistress: our nuptial day holds.

BEATRICE
With happy constancy a wishèd day.

[Exit.

FREEVILL
Myself and all content rest with you.

[Enter **MALHEUREUX**.

MALHEUREUX
The studious morn, with paler cheek, draws on
The day's bold light. Hark how the free-born birds
Carol their unaffected passions!

[The nightingales sing.

Now sing they sonnets—thus they cry, We love!
O breath of heaven! thus they, harmless souls,
Give entertain to mutual affects.
They have no bawds, no mercenary beds,
No polite restraints, no artificial heats,
No faint dissemblings; no custom makes them blush,
No shame afflicts their name. O you happy beasts!
In whom an inborn heat is not held sin,
How far transcend you wretched, wretched man,

Whom national custom, tyrannous respects
Of slavish order, fetters, lames his power,
Calling that sin in us which in all things else
Is Nature's highest virtue.
O miseri quorum gaudia crimen habent!
Sure Nature against virtue cross doth fall,
Or virtue's self is oft unnatural.
That I should love a strumpet! I, a man of snow!
Now, shame forsake me—whither am I fallen!
A creature of a public use! my friend's love, too!
To live to be a talk to men—a shame
To my professed virtue! O accursed reason,
How many eyes hast thou to see thy shame,
And yet how blind once to prevent defame!

FREEVILL

Diaboli virtus in lumbis est! Morrow, my friend. Come, I could make a tedious scene of this now; but what—Pah! thou art in love with a courtezan! Why, sir, should we loathe all strumpets, some men should hate their own mothers or sisters: a sin against kind, I can tell you.

MALHEUREUX

May it beseem a wise man to be in love?

FREEVILL

Let wise men alone, 'twill beseem thee and me well enough.

MALHEUREUX

Shall I not offend the vowed band of our friendship?

FREEVILL

What, to affect that which thy friend affected? By Heaven, I resign her freely; the creature and I must grow off; by this time she has assuredly heard of my resolved marriage, and no question swears "God's sacrament, ten towsand divells." I'll resign, i'faith.

MALHEUREUX

I would but embrace her, hear her speak, and at the most, but kiss her.

FREEVILL

O friend, he that could live with the smoke of roast-meat might live at a cheap rate!

MALHEUREUX

I shall ne'er prove heartily received;
A kind of flat ungracious modesty,
An insufficient dulness stains my 'haviour.

FREEVILL

No matter, sir; insufficiency and sottishness are much commendable in a most discommendable action: now could I swallow thee, thou hadst wont to be so harsh and cold: I'll tell thee,—hell and the prodigies of angry Jove are not so fearful to a thinking mind as a man without affection. Why, friend, philosophy and nature are all one; love is the centre in which all lines close, the common bond of being.

MALHEUREUX
O but a chaste reservèd privateness,
A modest continence!

FREEVILL
I'll tell thee what, take this as firmest sense:—
Incontinence will force a continence;
Heat wasteth heat, light defaceth light,
Nothing is spoiled but by his proper might.
This is something too weighty for thy floor.

MALHEUREUX
But howsoe'er you shade it, the world's eye
Shines hot and open on't;
Lying, malice, envy, are held but slidings,
Errors of rage, when custom and the world
Calls lust a crime spotted with blackest terrors.

FREEVILL
Where errors are held crimes, crimes are but errors.
Along, sir, to her; she's an arrant strumpet; and a strumpet is a sarpego, venom'd gonorrhy to man—things actually possessed—

[Offers to go out, and suddenly draws back.

—yet since thou art in love,—and again, as good make use of a statue—a body without a soul, a carcass three months dead—yet since thou art in love—

MALHEUREUX
Death, man! my destiny I cannot choose.

FREEVILL
Nay, I hope so. Again, they sell but only flesh,
No jot affection; so that even in the enjoying,
Absentem marmoreamque putes. Yet since you needs must love—

MALHEUREUX
Unavoidable, though folly—worse than madness!

FREEVILL
It's true; but since you needs must love, you must know this,—
He that must love, a fool and he must kiss.

[Enter **COCLEDEMOY**.

Master Cocledemoy, ut vales, Domine!

COCLEDEMOY
Ago tibi gratias, my worshipful friend, how does your friend?

FREEVILL
Out, you rascal!

COCLEDEMOY
Hang toasts, you are an ass; much o' your worship's brain lies in your calves; bread o' god, boy, I was at supper last night with a new-wean'd bulchin; bread o' god, drunk, horribly drunk—horribly drunk! there was a wench, one Frank Frailty, a punk, an honest polecat, of a clean instep, sound leg, smooth thigh, and the nimble devil in her buttock. Ah, feast o' grace! when saw you, Tysefew, or Master Caqueteur, that prattling gallant of a good draught, common customs, fortunate impudence, and sound fart?

FREEVILL
Away, rogue!

COCLEDEMOY
Hang toasts, my fine boy, my companion as worshipful.

MALHEUREUX
Yes, I hear you are taken up with scholars and churchmen.

[Enter **HOLIFERNES** the barber.

COCLEDEMOY
Quanquam te, Marce, fili, my fine boy.

HOLIFERNES
Does your worship want a barber-surgeon?

FREEVILL
Farewell, knave; beware the Mulligrubs.

[Exeunt **FREEVILL** and **MALHEREUX**.

COCLEDEMOY
Let the Mulligrubs beware the knave. What, a barber-surgeon, my delicate boy?

HOLIFERNES
Yes, sir, an apprentice to surgery.

COCLEDEMOY
'Tis, my fine boy. To what bawdy-house doth your master belong? What's thy name?

HOLIFERNES
Holifernes Reinscure.

COCLEDEMOY
Reinscure! Good Master Holifernes, I desire your further acquaintance; nay, pray ye be covered, my fine boy: kill thy itch, and heal thy scabs. Is thy master rotten?

HOLIFERNES
My father, forsooth, is dead—

COCLEDEMOY
And laid in his grave.
Alas! what comfort shall Peggy then have!

HOLIFERNES
None but me, sir; that's my mother's son, I assure you.

COCLEDEMOY
Mother's son? A good witty boy, would live to read an homily well: and to whom are you going now?

HOLIFERNES
Marry, forsooth, to trim Master Mulligrub the vintner.

COCLEDEMOY
Do you know Master Mulligrub?

HOLIFERNES
My godfather, sir.

COCLEDEMOY
Good boy: hold up thy chops. I pray thee do one thing for me: my name is Gudgeon.

HOLIFERNES
Good Master Gudgeon.

COCLEDEMOY
Lend me thy basin, razor, and apron.

HOLIFERNES
O Lord, sir!

COCLEDEMOY
Well spoken; good English. But what's thy furniture worth?

HOLIFERNES
O Lord, sir, I know not.

COCLEDEMOY
Well spoken; a boy of a good wit: hold this pawn; where dost dwell?

HOLIFERNES

At the sign of the Three Razors, sir.

COCLEDEMOY

A sign of good shaving, my catastrophonical fine boy. I have an odd jest to trim Master Mulligrub, for a wager; a jest, boy; a humour. I'll return thy things presently. Hold!

HOLIFERNES

What mean you, good Master Gudgeon?

COCLEDEMOY

Nothing, faith, but a jest, boy: drink that; I'll recoil presently.

HOLIFERNES

You'll not stay long.

COCLEDEMOY

As I am an honest man. The Three Razors?

HOLIFERNES

Ay, sir.

[Exit **HOLIFERNES**.

COCLEDEMOY

Good; and if I shave not Master Mulligrub, my wit has no edge, and I may go cack in my pewter. Let me see,—a barber: my scurvy tongue will discover me: must dissemble, must disguise; for my beard, my false hair; for my tongue—Spanish, Dutch or Welsh—no, a Northern barber; very good. Widow Reinscure's man, well; newly entertain'd, right; so, hang toasts! all cards have white backs, and all knaves would seem to have white breasts: so proceed now, worshipful Cocledemoy.

[Exit **COCLEDEMOY**, in his barber's furniture.

SCENE II

Franceschina's lodging.

Enter **MARY FAUGH**, and **FRANCESCHINA** with her hair loose, chafing.

MARY FAUGH

Nay, good sweet daughter, do not swagger so; you hear your love is to be married, true; he does cast you off, right; he will leave you to the world,—what then? though blue and white, black and green, leave you, may not red and yellow entertain you? is there but one colour in the rainbow?

FRANCESCHINA

Grand grincome on your sentences! God's sacrament, ten towsand divels take you!—you ha' brought mine love, mine honour, mine body, all to noting!

MARY FAUGH
To nothing! I'll be sworn I have brought them to all the things I could; I ha' made as much o' your maidenhead—and you had been mine own daughter, I could not ha' sold your maidenhead oft'ner than I ha' done. I ha' sworn for you, God forgive me! I have made you acquainted with the Spaniard, Don Skirtoll,—with the Italian, Messer Beieroane,—with the Irish lord, S. Patrick,—with the Dutch merchant, Haunce Herkin Glukin Skellam Flapdragon,—and specially with the greatest French, and now lastly with this English, yet, in my conscience, an honest gentleman. And am I now grown one of the accursed with you for my labour? Is this my reward? Am I call'd bawd? Well, Mary Faugh, go thy ways, Mary Faugh; thy kind heart will bring thee to the hospital.

FRANCESCHINA
Nay, good naunt, you'll help me to an oder love, vil you not?

MARY FAUGH
Out, thou naughty belly! wouldst thou make me thy bawd?—thou'st best make me thy bawd. I ha' kept counsel for thee: who paid the apothecary,—was't not honest Mary Faugh? who redeem'd thy petticoat and mantle,—was't not honest Mary Faugh? who helped thee to thy custom,—not swaggering Ireland captains, nor of two-shilling inns-o'-court men,—but with honest flat-caps, wealthy flat-caps, that pay for their pleasure the best of any men in Europe, nay, which is more, in London? And dost thou defy me, vile creature?

FRANCESCHINA
Foutra pon you,—vitch, bawd, polecat,—paugh! Did not you praise Freevill to mine love?

MARY FAUGH
I did praise, I confess, I did praise him; I said he was a fool, an unthrift, a true whoremaster, I confess; a constant drab-keeper, I confess: but what, the wind is turn'd!

FRANCESCHINA
It is, it is, vile woman!—reprobate woman!—naughty woman! it is: vat sall become of mine poor flesh now? mine body must turn Turk for twopence. O Divela, life o' mine art! ick sall be reveng'd!—do ten thousand hell damn me, ick sall have the rogue trote cut! and his love, and his friend, and all his affinity, sall smart! sall dye! sall hang! Now legion of devil seize him!—de gran pest, St. Anthony's fire, and de hot Neapolitan poc, rot him!

[Enter **FREEVILL** and **MALHEUREUX**.

FREEVILL
Franceschina!

FRANCESCHINA
O mine seet, dear'st, kindest, mine loving! O mine towsand, ten towsand, delicated, petty seet art!

[Cantat **GALLICÈ**.

Ah mine, ah dear leevest affection!

FREEVILL
Why, monkey, no fashion in you! Give entertain to my friend.

FRANCESCHINA
Ick sall make de most of you dat courtesy may. Aunt Mary, Mettre Faugh, stools, stools, for des gallants! Mine mettre sing non oder song,—frolic, frolic, sir!—but still complain me do her wrong. Lighten your heart, sir; for me did but kiss her,—for me did but kiss her—and so let go. Your friend is very heavy; ick sall ne'er like such sad company.

FREEVILL
No, thou delightest only in light company.

FRANCESCHINA
By mine trot, he been very sad; vat ail you, sir?

MALHEUREUX
A tooth-ache, lady, a paltry rheum.

FRANCESCHINA
De diet is very goot for de rheum.

FREEVILL
How far off dwells the house-surgeon, Mary Faugh?

MARY FAUGH
You are a profane fellow, i'faith; I little thought to hear such ungodly terms come from your lips.

FRANCESCHINA
Pre de now, 'tis but a toy, a very trifle.

FREEVILL
I care not for the value, Frank, but i'faith—

FRANCESCHINA
I'fait, me must needs have it (dis is Beatrice' ring, oh could I get it!); seet, pre de now, as ever you have embraced me with a hearty arm, a warm thought, or a pleasing touch, as ever you will profess to love me, as ever you do wish me life, give me dis ring, dis little ring.

FREEVILL
Prithee be not uncivilly importunate; sha' not ha't; faith, I care not for thee, nor thy jealousy; sha' not ha't, i'faith.

FRANCESCHINA
You do not love me. I hear of Sir Hubert Subboys' daughter, Mistress Beatrice. God's sacrament, ick could scratch out her eyes, and suck the holes!

FREEVILL

Go; y' are grown a punk rampant!
So, get thee gone; ne'er more behold min eyes, by thee made wretched!

FREEVILL

Mary Faugh, farewell!—farewell, Frank!

FRANCESCHINA

Sall I not ha' de ring?

FREEVILL

No, by the Lord!

FRANCESCHINA

By te Lord?

FREEVILL

By the Lord!

FRANCESCHINA

Go to your new blouze,—your unproved sluttery,—your modest mettre, forsooth!

FREEVILL

Marry, will I, forsooth!

FRANCESCHINA

Will you marry, forsooth?

FREEVILL

Do not turn witch before thy time.—
With all my heart, sir, you will stay.

MALHEUREUX

I am no whit myself. Video meliora proboque,
But raging lust my fate all strong doth move;
The gods themselves cannot be wise and love.

FREEVILL

Your wishes to you!

[Exit **FREEVILL**.

MALHEUREUX

Beauty entirely choice—

FRANCESCHINA

Pray ye prove a man of fashion, and neglect the neglected.

MALHEUREUX

Can such a rarity be neglected?—can there be measure or sin in loving such a creature?

FRANCESCHINA

O min poor forsaken heart!

MALHEUREUX

I cannot contain,—he saw thee not that left thee.
If there be wisdom, reason, honour, grace,
Of any foolishly-esteemèd virtue,
In giving o'er possession of such beauty,
Let me be vicious, so I may be loved.
Passion, I am thy slave; sweet, it shall be my grace,
That I account thy love my only virtue:
Shall I swear I am thy most vowèd servant?

FRANCESCHINA

Mine vowed? Go! go! go! I cannot more of love. No! no! no! You bin all unconstant. O unfaithful men—
tyrants—betrayers—de very enjoying us loseth us; and when you only ha' made us hateful, you only
hate us. O mine forsaken heart!

MALHEUREUX

I must not rave. Silence and modesty two customary virtues. Will you be my mistress?

FRANCESCHINA

Mettres? Ha! ha! ha!

MALHEUREUX

Will you lie with me?

FRANCESCHINA

Lie with you? O no; you men will out-lie any woman; fait, me no more can love.

MALHEUREUX

No matter, let me enjoy your bed.

FRANCESCHINA

O! vile man, vat do you tinck on me? Do you take me to be a beast—a creature that for sense only will
entertain love, and not only for love—love? O! brutish abomination!

MALHEUREUX

Why, then I pray thee love, and with thy love enjoy me—

FRANCESCHINA

Give me reason to affect you. Will you swear you love me?

MALHEUREUX

So seriously, that I protest no office so dangerous—no deed so unreasonable—no cost so heavy, but I vow to the utmost tentation of my best being to effect it.

FRANCESCHINA
Sall I, or can I trust again? O fool!
How natural 'tis for us to be abused!
Sall ick be sure that no satiety,
No enjoying,
Not time shall languish your affection?

MALHEUREUX
If there be ought in brain, heart, or hand,
Can make you doubtless, I am your vow'd servant.

FRANCESCHINA
Will you do one ting for me?

MALHEUREUX
Can I do it?

FRANCESCHINA
Yes, yes; but ick do not love dis same Freevill.

MALHEUREUX
Well?

FRANCESCHINA
Nay, I do hate him.

MALHEUREUX
So.

FRANCESCHINA
By this kiss I hate him.

MALHEUREUX
I love to feel such oaths; swear again.

FRANCESCHINA
No, no. Did you ever hear of any that loved at the first sight?

MALHEUREUX
A thing most proper.

FRANCESCHINA
Now fait, I judge it all incredible until this hour I saw you: pretty fair-eyed yout, would you enjoy me?

MALHEUREUX

Rather than my breath, even as my being.

FRANCESCHINA
Vel! had ick not made a vow—

MALHEUREUX
What vow?

FRANCESCHINA
O let me forget it; it makes us both despair!

MALHEUREUX
Dear soul, what vow?

FRANCESCHINA
Ha, good morrow, gentle sir; endeavour to forget me, as I must be enforced to forget all men. Sweet mind rest in you.

MALHEUREUX
Stay, let not thy desire burst me. O my impatient heat endures no resistance—no protraction! there is no being for me but your sudden enjoying.

FRANCESCHINA
I do not love Freevill.

MALHEUREUX
But what vow? what vow?

FRANCESCHINA
So long as Freevill lives, I must not love.

MALHEUREUX
Then he—

FRANCESCHINA
Must—

MALHEUREUX
Die!

FRANCESCHINA
I know there is no such vehemence in your affects.
Would I were anything, so he were not!

MALHEUREUX
Will you be mine when he is not?

FRANCESCHINA

Will I? Dear, dear breast, by this most zealous kiss! but I will not persuade you; but if you hate him that I loathe most deadly; yet as you please—I'll persuade noting.

MALHEUREUX
Will you be only mine?

FRANCESCHINA
Vill I? How hard 'tis for true love to dissemble.
I am only yours.

MALHEUREUX
'Tis as irrevocable as breath: he dies.
Your love!

FRANCESCHINA
My vow,—not until he be dead;
Which that I may be sure not to infringe,
Dis token of his death sall satisfy:
He has a ring, as dear as the air to him,
His new love's gift; tat got and brought to me,
I shall assurèd your professèd rest.

MALHEUREUX
To kill a man?

FRANCESCHINA
O! done safely; a quarrel sudden pick'd,
With an advantage strike—then bribe—a little coin,
All's safe, dear soul; but I'll not set you on.

MALHEUREUX
Nay, he is gone—the ring! Well, come, little more liberal of thy love.

FRANCESCHINA
Not yet; my vow.

MALHEUREUX
O Heaven! there is no hell but love's prolongings.
Dear, farewell.

FRANCESCHINA
Farewell.
Now does my heart swell high, for my revenge
Has birth and form; first friend sall kill his friend.
He dat survives I'll hang; besides de chaste
Beatrice I'll vex. Only de ring;
Dat got, the world sall know the worst of evils:
Woman corrupted is the worst of devils.

[Exit **FRANCESCHINA**.

MALHEUREUX
To kill my friend! O 'tis to kill myself!
Yet man's but man's excrement—man breeding man
As he does worms; or this, to spoil this nothing.

[He spits.

The body of a man is of the self-same mould
As ox or horse; no murder to kill these.
As for that only part which makes us man,
Murder wants power to touch't. O wit, how vile!
How hellish art thou, when thou raisest nature
'Gainst sacred faith! Think more: to kill a friend
To gain a woman! to lose a virtuous self
For appetite and sensual end, whose very having
Loseth all appetite, and gives satiety!
That corporal end, remorse and inward blushings,
Forcing us loathe the steam of our own heats;
Whilst friendship closed in virtue, being spiritual,
Tastes no such languishings, and moments' pleasure
With much repentance; but like rivers flow,
And further that they run they bigger grow.
Lord, how was I misgone! how easy 'tis to err,
When passion will not give us leave to think!
A learn'd, that is an honest man, may fear,
And lust, and rage, and malice, and anything,
When he is taken uncollected suddenly:
'Tis sin of cold blood, mischief with waked eyes,
That is the damnèd and the truly vice;
Not he that's passionless, but he 'bove passion's wise.
My friend shall know it all.

[Exit.

SCENE III

A Tavern.

Enter **MASTER MULLIGRUB** and **MISTRESS MULLIGRUB**, she with a bag of money.

MISTRESS MULLIGRUB
It is right, I assure you, just fifteen pounds.

MULLIGRUB

Well, Cocledemoy, 'tis thou putt'st me to this charge; but, and I catch thee, I'll charge thee with as many irons. Well, is the barber come? I'll be trimm'd, and then to Cheapside to buy a fair piece of plate, to furnish the loss. Is the barber come?

MISTRESS MULLIGRUB

Truth, husband, surely heaven is not pleased with our vocation. We do wink at the sins of our people. Our wines are protestants; and I speak it to my grief, and to the burthen of my conscience, we fry our fish with salt butter.

MULLIGRUB

Go, look to your business; mend the matter, and score false with a vengeance.

[Exit **MISTRESS MULLIGRUB**.

[Enter **COCLEDEMOY** like a barber.

Welcome, friend, whose man?

COCLEDEMOY

Widow Reinscure's man; and shall please your good worship, my name's Andrew Shark.

MULLIGRUB

How does my godson, good Andrew?

COCLEDEMOY

Very well, he's gone to trim Master Quicquid, our parson. Hold up your head.

MULLIGRUB

How long have you been a barber, Andrew?

COCLEDEMOY

Not long, sir; this two year.

MULLIGRUB

What! and a good workman already. I dare scarce trust my head to thee.

COCLEDEMOY

O, fear not; we ha' poll'd better men than you; we learn the trade very quickly. Will your good worship be shaven or cut?

MULLIGRUB

As you will. What trade didst live by before thou turnedst barber, Andrew?

COCLEDEMOY

I was a pedlar in Germany; but my countrymen thrive better by this trade.

MULLIGRUB

What's the news, barber? thou art sometimes at court.

COCLEDEMOY
Sometimes poll a page or so, sir.

MULLIGRUB
And what's the news? How do all my good lords and all my good ladies, and all the rest of my acquaintance?

COCLEDEMOY
What an arrogant knave's this! I'll acquaintance ye! 'Tis cash!—

[He spieth the bag.

—Say ye, sir?

MULLIGRUB
And what news—what news, good Andrew?

COCLEDEMOY
Marry, sir, you know the Conduit at Greenwich, and the under-holes that spouts up water?

MULLIGRUB
Very well; I was wash'd there one day, and so was my wife—you might have wrung her smock, i'faith! But what o' those holes?

COCLEDEMOY
Thus, sir. Out of those little holes, in the midst of the night, crawl'd out twenty-four huge, horrible, monstrous, fearful, devouring—

MULLIGRUB
Bless us!

COCLEDEMOY
Serpents, which no sooner were beheld, but they turn'd to mastiffs, which howl'd; those mastiffs instantly turn'd to cocks, which crowed; those cocks, in a moment, were changed to bears, which roar'd; which bears are at this hour to be yet seen in Paris Garden, living upon nothing but toasted cheese and green onions.

MULLIGRUB
By the Lord! and this may be, my wife and I will go see them. This portends something.

COCLEDEMOY [Aside]
Yes, worshipful fist, thou'st feel what portends by and by.

MULLIGRUB
And what more news? You shave the world—especially you barber-surgeons—you know the ground of many things. You are cunning privy searchers: by the mass, you scour all. What more news?

COCLEDEMOY

They say, sir, that twenty-five couple of Spanish jennets are to be seen, hand in hand, dance the old measures, whilst six goodly Flaunders mares play to them on a noise of flutes.

MULLIGRUB

O monstrous! this is a lie o' my word. Nay, and this be not a lie—I am no fool, I warrant—nay, make an ass of me once?

COCLEDEMOY

Shut your eyes close—wink; sure, sir, this ball will make you smart.

MULLIGRUB

I do wink.

COCLEDEMOY

Your head will take cold;

[**COCLEDEMOY** puts on a coxcomb on **MULLIGRUB'S** head.

I will put on your good worship's nightcap whilst I shave you. So, mum, hang toasts! Faugh, via! sparrows must peck and Cocledemoy munch.

MULLIGRUB

Ha, ha, ha! Twenty-five couple of Spanish jennets to dance the old measures. Andrew makes my worship laugh, i'faith. Dost take me for an ass, Andrew?—dost know one Cocledemoy in town? He made me an ass last night, but I'll ass him! Art thou free, Andrew? Shave me well—I shall be one of the common council shortly—and then, Andrew—why, Andrew, Andrew, dost leave me in the suds?

[Cantat.

Why, Andrew, I shall be blind with winking. Ha! Andrew—wife—Andrew, what means this? Wife!—my money, wife!

[Enter **MISTRESS MULLIGRUB**.

MISTRESS MULLIGRUB

What's the noise with you? What ail you?

MULLIGRUB

Where's the barber?

MISTRESS MULLIGRUB

Gone. I saw him depart long since. Why, are not you trimm'd?

MULLIGRUB

Trimm'd! O wife! I am shaved. Did you take hence the money?

MISTRESS MULLIGRUB

I touch'd it not, as I am religious.

MULLIGRUB

O Lord! I have wink'd fair.

[Enter **HOLIFERNES**.

HOLIFERNES

I pray, godfather, give me your blessing.

MULLIGRUB

O Holifernes—O where's thy mother's Andrew?

HOLIFERNES

Blessing, godfather!

MULLIGRUB

The devil choke thee! where's Andrew, thy mother's man?

HOLIFERNES

My mother hath none such, forsooth.

MULLIGRUB

My money—fifteen pounds—plague of all Andrews! who was't trimm'd me?

HOLIFERNES

I know not, godfather; only one met me, as I was coming to you, and borrowed my furniture, as he said, for a jest' sake.

MULLIGRUB

What kind of fellow?

HOLIFERNES

A thick, elderly, stub-bearded fellow.

MULLIGRUB

Cocledemoy, Cocledemoy! Raise all the wise men in the street! I'll hang him with mine own hands! O wife! some rosa solis.

MISTRESS MULLIGRUB

Good husband, take comfort in the Lord; I'll play the devil, but I'll recover it. Have a good conscience, 'tis but a week's cutting in the term!

MULLIGRUB

O, wife! O, wife! O, Jack! how does thy mother? Is there any fiddlers in the house?

MISTRESS MULLIGRUB

Yes, Master Creak's noise?

MULLIGRUB
Bid 'em play, laugh, make merry; cast up my accounts, for I'll go hang myself presently. I will not curse, but a pox on Cocledemoy; he has poll'd and shaved me, he has trimm'd me!

[Exeunt.

ACT III

SCENE I

Room in Sir Hubert Subboys' house.

Enter **BEATRICE**, **CRISPINELLA** and **NURSE PUTIFER**.

PUTIFER
Nay, good child o' love, once more Master Freevill's sonnet o' the kiss you gave him.

BEATRICE
Sha't, good nurse:

[SINGS.
Purest lips, soft banks of blisses,
Self alone deserving kisses;
O give me leave to, &c.

CRISPINELLA
Pish! sister Beatrice, prithee read no more; my stomach o' late stands against kissing extremely.

BEATRICE
Why, good Crispinella?

CRISPINELLA
By the faith and trust I bear to my face, 'tis grown one of the most unsavoury ceremonies: body o' beauty! 'tis one of the most unpleasing injurious customs to ladies: any fellow that has but one nose on his face, and standing collar and skirts also lined with taffety sarcenet, must salute us on the lips as familiarly—Soft skins save us! there was a stub-bearded John-a-Stile with a ployden's face saluted me last day and struck his bristles through my lips; I ha' spent ten shillings in pomatum since to skin them again. Marry, if a nobleman or a knight with one lock visit us, though his unclean goose-turd-green teeth ha' the palsy, his nostrils smell worse than a putrified marrowbone, and his loose beard drops into our bosom, yet we must kiss him with a cursy, a curse! for my part, I had as lieve they would break wind in my lips.

BEATRICE
Fie, Crispinella, you speak too broad.

CRISPINELLA

No jot, sister; let's ne'er be ashamed to speak what we be not ashamed to think: I dare as boldly speak venery as think venery.

BEATRICE

Faith, sister! I'll begone if you speak so broad.

CRISPINELLA

Will you so? Now bashfulness seize you, we pronounce boldly, robbery, murder, treason, which deeds must needs be far more loathsome than an act which is so natural, just, and necessary, as that of procreation; you shall have an hypocritical vestal virgin speak that with close teeth publicly, which she will receive with open mouth privately; for my own part, I consider nature without apparel; without disguising of custom or compliment, I give thoughts words, and words truth, and truth boldness; she whose honest freeness makes it her virtue to speak what she thinks will make it her necessity to think what is good. I love no prohibited things, and yet I would have nothing prohibited by policy, but by virtue; for as in the fashion of time those books that are call'd in are most in sale and request, so in nature those actions that are most prohibited are most desired.

BEATRICE

Good quick sister, stay your pace; we are private, but the world would censure you, for truly severe modesty is women's virtue.

CRISPINELLA

Fie, fie! virtue is a free, pleasant, buxom quality. I love a constant countenance well; but this froward ignorant coyness, sour austere lumpish uncivil privateness, that promises nothing but rough skins and hard stools; ha! fie on't, good for nothing but for nothing. Well, nurse, and what do you conceive of all this?

PUTIFER

Nay, faith, my conceiving days be done. Marry for kissing, I'll defend that; that's within my compass; but for my own part, here's Mistress Beatrice is to be married with the grace of God; a fine gentleman he is shall have her, and I warrant a strong; he has a leg like a post, a nose like a lion, a brow like a bull, and a beard of most fair expectation: this week you must marry him, and I now will read a lecture to you both, how you shall behave yourselves to your husbands the first month of your nuptial; I ha' broke my skull about it, I can tell you, and there is much brain in it.

CRISPINELLA

Read it to my sister, good nurse, for I assure you I'll ne'er marry.

PUTIFER

Marry, God forfend, what will you do then?

CRISPINELLA

Faith, strive against the flesh. Marry! no, faith, husbands are like lots in the lottery: you may draw forty blanks before you find one that has any prize in him. A husband generally is a careless, domineering thing, that grows like coral, which as long as it is under water is soft and tender, but as soon as it has got his branch above the waves is presently hard, stiff, not to be bowed but burst; so when your husband is a suitor and under your choice, Lord how supple he is, how obsequious, how at your service, sweet lady! Once married, got up his head above, a stiff, crooked, nobby, inflexible tyrannous creature he grows; then they turn like water, more you would embrace the less you hold. I'll live my own woman, and if the worst come to the worst, I had rather prove a wag than a fool.

BEATRICE
O, but a virtuous marriage.

CRISPINELLA
Virtuous marriage! there is no more affinity betwixt virtue and marriage than betwixt a man and his horse; indeed virtue gets up upon marriage sometimes, and manageth it in the right way; but marriage is of another piece, for as a horse may be without a man, and a man without a horse, so marriage, you know, is often without virtue, and virtue, I am sure, more oft without marriage. But thy match, sister— by my troth I think 'twill do well; he's a well-shaped, clean-lipp'd gentleman, of a handsome, but not affected, fineness, a good faithful eye, and a well-humour'd cheek; would he did not stoop in the shoulders, for thy sake. See, here he is.

[Enter **FREEVILL** and **TYSEFEW**.

FREEVILL
Good day, sweet!

CRISPINELLA
Good morrow, brother! nay, you shall have my lip. Good morrow, servant!

TYSEFEW
Good morrow, sweet life!

CRISPINELLA
Life! dost call thy mistress life?

TYSEFEW
Life! yes, why not life?

CRISPINELLA
How many mistresses hast thou?

TYSEFEW
Some nine.

CRISPINELLA
Why then thou hast nine lives, like a cat.

TYSEFEW
Mew, you would be taken up for that.

CRISPINELLA
Nay, good, let me still sit; we low statures love still to sit, lest when we stand we may be supposed to sit.

TYSEFEW
Dost not wear high cork shoes—chopines?

CRISPINELLA
Monstrous ones: I am, as many other are, pieced above and pieced beneath.

TYSEFEW
Still the best part in the—

CRISPINELLA
And yet all will scarce make me so high as one of the giants' stilts that stalks before my Lord Mayor's pageant:

TYSEFEW
By the Lord, so I thought 'twas for something Mistress Joyce jested at thy high insteps.

CRISPINELLA
She might well enough, and long enough, before I would be ashamed of my shortness: what I made or can mend myself I may blush at; but what nature put upon me, let her be ashamed for me, I ha' nothing to do with it. I forget my beauty.

TYSEFEW
Faith, Joyce is a foolish bitter creature.

CRISPINELLA
A pretty mildewed wench she is.

TYSEFEW
And fair—

CRISPINELLA
As myself!

TYSEFEW
O you forget your beauty now.

CRISPINELLA
Troth, I never remember my beauty, but as some men do religion,—for controversy's sake.

BEATRICE
A motion, sister.

CRISPINELLA
Nineveh, Julius Cæsar, Jonas, or the destruction of Jerusalem.

BEATRICE
My love, hear.

CRISPINELLA
Prithee call him not love, 'tis the drab's phrase: nor sweet honey, nor my coney, nor dear duckling, they are citizen terms, but call him—

BEATRICE
What?

CRISPINELLA
Anything.—What's the motion?

BEATRICE
You know this night our parents have intended solemnly to contract us, and my love, to grace the feast, hath promised a masque.

FREEVILL
You'll make one, Tysefew, and Caqueteur shall fill up a room.

TYSEFEW
'Fore heaven, well-remember'd; he borrowed a diamond of me last night to grace his finger in your visitation. The lying creature will swear some strange thing on it now.

[Enter **CAQUETEUR**.

CRISPINELLA
Peace, he's here; stand close, lurk.

CAQUETEUR
Good morrow, most dear, and worthy to be most wise. How does my mistress?

CRISPINELLA
Morrow, sweet servant; you glister,—prithee, let's see that stone.

CAQUETEUR
A toy, lady, I bought to please my finger.

CRISPINELLA
Why, I am more precious to you than your finger.

CAQUETEUR
Yes, or than all my body, I swear.

CRISPINELLA
Why, then let it be bought to please me; come, I am no professed beggar.

CAQUETEUR
Troth, mistress! Zoons! Forsooth, I protest!

CRISPINELLA

Nay, if you turn Protestant for such a toy.

CAQUETEUR

In good deed, la; another time I'll give you a—

CRISPINELLA

Is this yours to give?

CAQUETEUR

O God! forsooth mine, quoth you; nay, as for that—

CRISPINELLA

Now I remember, I ha' seen this on my servant Tysefew's finger.

CAQUETEUR

Such another.

CRISPINELLA

Nay, I am sure this is it.

CAQUETEUR

Troth, 'tis forsooth. The poor fellow wanted money to pay for supper last night, and so pawn'd it to me; 'tis a pawn, i'faith, or else you should have it.

TYSEFEW

Hark ye, thou base lying—How dares thy impudence hope to prosper? Were't not for the privilege of this respected company, I would so bang thee.

CRISPINELLA

Come hither, servant. What's the matter betwixt you two?

CAQUETEUR

Nothing; but hark you, he did me some uncivil discourtesies last night; for which, because I should not call him to account, he desires to make me any satisfaction. The coward trembles at my very presence; but I ha' him on the hip; I'll take the forfeit on his ring.

TYSEFEW

What's that you whisper to her?

CAQUETEUR

Nothing, sir; but satisfy her that the ring was not pawn'd, but only lent by you to grace my finger; and so told her I craved pardon for being too familiar, or indeed over-bold with your reputation.

CRISPINELLA

Yes, indeed, he did. He said you desired to make him any satisfaction for an uncivil discourtesy you did him last night; but he said he had you o' the hip, and would take the forfeit of your ring.

TYSEFEW

How now, ye base poltroon.

CAQUETEUR

Hold! hold! my mistress speaks by contraries.

TYSEFEW

Contraries!

CAQUETEUR

She jests—faith, only jests.

CRISPINELLA

Sir, I'll no more o' your service—you are a child—I'll give you to my nurse.

PUTIFER

And he come to me, I can tell you, as old as I am, what to do with him.

CAQUETEUR

I offer my service, forsooth.

TYSEFEW

Why, so: now, every dog has his bone to gnaw on.

FREEVILL

The masque holds, Master Caqueteur.

CAQUETEUR

I am ready, sir. Mistress, I'll dance with you, ne'er fear—I'll grace you.

PUTIFER

I tell you, I can my singles and my doubles, and my trick o' twenty—my carantapace—my traverse forward—and my falling back, yet, i'faith.

BEATRICE

Mine! The provision for the night is ours. Much must be our care; till night we leave you; I am your servant, be not tyrannous. Your virtue won me; faith, my love's not lust; Good, wrong me not; my most fault is much trust.

FREEVILL

Until night only, my heart be with you. Farewell, sister.

CRISPINELLA

Adieu, brother. Come on, sister, for these sweetmeats.

FREEVILL

Let's meet and practise presently.

TYSEFEW
Content; we'll but fit our pumps. Come, ye pernicious vermin.

[Exeunt **ALL** but **FREEVILL**.

[Enter **MALHEUREUX**.

FREEVILL
My friend, wished hours! What news from Babylon?
How does the woman of sin and natural concupiscence?

MALHEUREUX
The eldest child of nature ne'er beheld
So damn'd a creature.

FREEVILL
What! In nova fert animus mutatas dicere formas?
Which way bears the tide?

MALHEUREUX
Dear loved sir, I find a mind courageously vicious may be put on a desperate security; but can never be blessed with a firm enjoying and self-satisfaction.

FREEVILL
What passion is this, my dear Lindabrides?

MALHEUREUX
'Tis well; we both may jest; I ha' been tempted to your death.

FREEVILL
What, is the rampant cocatrice grown mad for the loss of her men?

MALHEUREUX
Devilishly mad.

FREEVILL
As most assured of my second love?

MALHEUREUX
Right.

FREEVILL
She would have had this ring.

MALHEUREUX
Ay, and this heart; and in true proof you were slain, I should bring her this ring, from which she was assured
You would not part until from life you parted;

For which deed, and only for which deed, I should possess her sweetness.

FREEVILL

O! bloody villains! Nothing is defamed but by his proper self. Physicians abuse remedies; lawyers spoil the law; and women only shame women. You ha' vow'd my death?

MALHEUREUX

My lust, not I, before my reason would; yet I must use her. That I, a man of sense, should conceive endless pleasure in a body whose soul I know to be so hideously black!

FREEVILL

That a man at twenty-three should cry, O sweet pleasure! and at forty-three should sigh, O sharp pox! But consider man furnished with omnipotence, and you overthrow him; thou must cool thy impatient appetite. 'Tis fate, 'tis fate!

MALHEUREUX

I do malign my creation that I am subject to passion. I must enjoy her.

FREEVILL

I have it, mark. I give a masque to-night
To my love's kindred; in that thou shalt go.
In that we two make show of falling out.
Give seeming challenge—instantly depart,
With some suspicion to present fight.
We will be seen as going to our swords;
And after meeting, this ring only lent,
I'll lurk in some obscure place, till rumour
(The common bawd to loose suspicions)
Have feign'd me slain, which (in respect myself
Will not be found, and our late seeming quarrel)
Will quickly sound to all as earnest truth.
Then to thy wench; protest me surely dead;
Show her this ring, enjoy her, and, blood cold,
We'll laugh at folly.

MALHEUREUX

O but think of it!

FREEVILL

Think of it! come away; virtue, let sleep thy passions;
What old times held as crimes, are now but fashions.

[Exeunt.

SCENE II

House of Master Burnish, the jeweller.

Enter **MASTER BURNISH** and **LIONEL. MASTER MULLIGRUB**, with a standing cup in his hand, and an obligation in the other. **COCLEDEMOY** stands at the other door, disguised like a French pedlar, and overhears them.

MULLIGRUB
I am not at this time furnish'd; but there's my bond for your plate.

BURNISH
Your bill had been sufficient: y'are a good man. A standing cup parcel-gilt of thirty-two ounces, eleven pounds seven shillings, the first of July. Good plate—good man—good day—good all.

MULLIGRUB
'Tis my hard fortune; I will hang the knave. No, first he shall half rot in fetters in the dungeon—his conscience made despairful. I'll hire a knave o' purpose—shall assure him he is damn'd; and after see him with mine own eyes, hang'd without singing any psalm. Lord, that he has but one neck!

BURNISH
You are too tyrannous;—you'll use me no further?

MULLIGRUB
No, sir; lend me your servant, only to carry the plate home. I have occasion of an hour's absence.

BURNISH
With easy consent, sir.—Haste and be careful.

[Exit **BURNISH**.

MULLIGRUB
Be very careful, I pray thee,—to my wife's own hands.

LIONEL
Secure yourself, sir.

MULLIGRUB
To her own hand!

LIONEL
Fear not, I have delivered greater things than this to a woman's own hand.

COCLEDEMOY
Mounsier, please you to buy a fine delicate ball, sweet ball—a camphor ball?

MULLIGRUB
Prithee, away!

[Exit **LIONEL**.

COCLEDEMOY
Wun' a ball to scour—a scouring ball—a ball to be shaved!

MULLIGRUB
For the love of God! talk not of shaving. I have been shaved—mischief and a thousand devils seize him!—I have been shaved!

[Exit **MULLIGRUB**.

COCLEDEMOY
The fox grows fat when he is cursed—I'll shave ye smoother yet. Turd on a tile stone! my lips have a kind of rheum at this bole. I'll have't—I'll gargalise my throat with this vintner, and when I have done with him, spit him out. I'll shark! Conscience does not repine. Were I to bite an honest gentleman, a poor grogaran poet, or a penurious parson that had but ten pigs' tails in a twelvemonth, and, for want of learning, had but one good stool in a fortnight, I were damn'd beyond the works of supererogation; but to wring the withers of my gouty-barm'd spiggod-frigging jumbler of elements, Mulligrub, I hold it as lawful as sheep-shearing, taking eggs from hens, caudles from asses, or butter'd shrimps from horses— they make no use of them, were not provided for them. And, therefore, worshipful Cocledemoy, hang toasts! On, in grace and virtue to proceed, only beware, beware degrees. There be rounds in a ladder, and knots in a halter; ware carts, hang toasts, the common council has decreed it! I must draw a lot for the great goblet.

[Exit.

SCENE III

A Tavern.

Enter Mistress Mulligrub, and Lionel with a goblet.

MISTRESS MULLIGRUB
Nay, I pray you, stay and drink; and how does your mistress? I know her very well—I have been inward with her, and so has many more. She was ever a good, patient creature, i'faith! With all my heart, I'll remember your master, an honest man. He knew me before I was married! An honest man he is, and a crafty. He comes forward in the world well, I warrant him; and his wife is a proper woman, that she is. Well, she has been as proper a woman as any in Cheap. She paints now, and yet she keeps her husband's old customers to him still. In troth, a fine-faced wife, in a wainscot-carved seat, is a worthy ornament to a tradesman's shop, and an attractive, I warrant; her husband shall find it in the custom of his ware, I'll assure him. God be with you, good youth; I acknowledge the receipt.

[Exit **LIONEL**.

I acknowledge all the receipt—sure, 'tis very well spoken—I acknowledge the receipt. Thus 'tis to have good education, and to be brought up in a tavern. I do keep as gallant and as good company, though I say it, as any she in London. Squires, gentlemen, and knights diet at my table, and I do lend some of them money; and full many fine men go upon my score, as simple as I stand here, and I trust them; and truly they very knightly and courtly promise fair, give me very good words, and a piece of flesh when time of year serves. Nay, though my husband be a citizen, and's cap's made of wool, yet I ha' wit, and can see my good as soon as another, for I have all the thanks; my silly husband, alas! he knows nothing of it; 'tis I that bear—'tis I that must bear a brain for all.

[Enter **COCLEDEMOY**.

COCLEDEMOY
Fair hour to you, mistress!

MISTRESS MULLIGRUB
Fair hour!—fine term!—faith, I'll score it up anon.—A beautiful thought to you, sir.

COCLEDEMOY
Your husband, and my master, Mr. Burnish, has sent you a jole of fresh salmon, and they both will come to dinner to season your new cup with the best wine, which cup your husband entreats you to send back by me, that his arms may be graved a' the side, which he forgot before it was sent.

MISTRESS MULLIGRUB
By what token are you sent?—by no token? Nay, I have wit.

COCLEDEMOY
He sent me by the same token, that he was dry shaved this morning.

MISTRESS MULLIGRUB
A sad token, but true. Here, sir, I pray you commend me to your master, but especially to your mistress. Tell them they shall be most sincerely welcome.

[Exit.

COCLEDEMOY
Shall be most sincerely welcome! Worshipful Cocledemoy, lurk close. Hang toasts! Be not ashamed of thy quality! Every man's turd smells well in's own nose. Vanish, foyst!

[Exit.

[Re-enter **MISTRESS MULLIGRUB**, with **SERVANTS** and furniture for the table.

MISTRESS MULLIGRUB
Come, spread these table diaper napkins, and—do you hear—perfume this parlour; does so smell of profane tobacco. I could never endure this ungodly tobacco, since one of our elders assured me, upon his knowledge, tobacco was not used in the congregation of the family of love. Spread, spread handsomely—Lord? these boys do things arsy-versy—you show your bringing up. I was a gentlewoman by my sister's side—I can tell ye so methodically. Methodically! I wonder where I got that word? O! Sir Aminadab Ruth bad me kiss him methodically!—I had it somewhere, and I had it indeed.

[Enter **MASTER MULLIGRUB**.

MULLIGRUB

Mind, be not desperate; I'll recover all.
All things with me shall seem honest that can be profitable,
He must ne'er winch, that would or thrive or save,
To be call'd niggard, cuckold, cut-throat, knave!

MISTRESS MULLIGRUB

Are they come, husband?

MULLIGRUB

Who?—what?—how now? What feast towards in my private parlour?

MISTRESS MULLIGRUB

Pray leave your foolery! What, are they come?

MULLIGRUB

Come—who come?

MISTRESS MULLIGRUB

You need not make't so strange!

MULLIGRUB

Strange?

MISTRESS MULLIGRUB

Ay, strange. You know no man that sent me word that he and his wife would come to dinner to me, and sent this jole of fresh salmon beforehand?

MULLIGRUB

Peace—not I—peace! The messenger hath mistaken the house; let's eat it up quickly before it be inquired for. Sit to it—some vinegar—quick! Some good luck yet. Faith, I never tasted salmon relish better! Oh! when a man feeds at other men's cost!

MISTRESS MULLIGRUB

Other men's cost! Why, did not you send this jole of salmon?

MULLIGRUB

No.

MISTRESS MULLIGRUB

By Master Burnish' man?

MULLIGRUB

No.

MISTRESS MULLIGRUB

Sending me word that he and his wife would come to dinner to me?

MULLIGRUB

No, no.

MISTRESS MULLIGRUB

To season my new bowl?

MULLIGRUB

Bowl!

MISTRESS MULLIGRUB

And withal will'd me to send the bowl back.

MULLIGRUB

Back!

MISTRESS MULLIGRUB

That you might have your arms graved on the side?

MULLIGRUB

Ha!

MISTRESS MULLIGRUB

By the same token you were dry-shaven this morning before you went forth.

MULLIGRUB

Pah! how this salmon stinks!

MISTRESS MULLIGRUB

And thereupon sent the bowl back, prepar'd dinner—nay, and I bear not a brain.

MULLIGRUB

Wife, do not vex me! Is the bowl gone?—is it deliver'd?

MISTRESS MULLIGRUB

Deliver'd! Yes, sure, 'tis deliver'd.

MULLIGRUB

I will never more say my prayers. Do not make me mad; 'tis common. Let me not cry like a woman. Is it gone?

MISTRESS MULLIGRUB

Gone? God is my witness, I deliver'd it with no more intention to be cozen'd on't than the child new born; and yet—

MULLIGRUB

Look to my house! I am haunted with evil spirits! Hear me; do hear me! If I have not my goblet again, heaven! I'll to the devil,—I'll to a conjurer. Look to my house! I'll raise all the wise men i' the street.

[Exit.

MISTRESS MULLIGRUB
Deliver us! What words are these? I trust in God he is but drunk, sure.

[Re-enter **COCLEDEMOY**.

COCLEDEMOY
I must have the salmon too; worshipful Cocledemoy, now for the masterpiece. God bless thy neckpiece, and foutra!—Fair mistress, my master—

MISTRESS MULLIGRUB
Have I caught you?—what, Roger?

COCLEDEMOY
Peace, good mistress. I'll tell you all. A jest; a very mere jest: your husband only took sport to fright you:—the bowl's at my master's; and there is your husband, who sent me in all haste lest you should be over-frighted with his feigning, to come to dinner to him.

MISTRESS MULLIGRUB
Praise heaven it is no worse.

COCLEDEMOY
And desired me to desire you to send the jole of salmon before, and yourself to come after to them; my mistress would be right glad to see you.

MISTRESS MULLIGRUB
I pray carry it. Now thank them entirely. Bless me, I was never so out of my skin in my life! pray thank your mistress most entirely.

COCLEDEMOY
So now, figo! worshipful Mall Faugh and I will munch; cheaters and bawds go together like washing and wringing.

[Exit.

MISTRESS MULLIGRUB
Beshrew his heart for his labour, how everything about me quivers. What, Christian! my hat and aporn: here, take my sleeves. And how I tremble! so I'll gossip it now for't, that's certain; here has been revolutions and false fires indeed.

[Enter **MULLIGRUB**.

MULLIGRUB
Whither now?—what's the matter with you now?—whither are you a-gadding?

MISTRESS MULLIGRUB

Come, come, play the fool no more. Will you go?

MULLIGRUB

Whither, in the rank name of madness—whither?

MISTRESS MULLIGRUB

Whither?—why to Master Burnish, to eat the jole of salmon. Lord, how strange you make it!

MULLIGRUB

Why so?—why so?

MISTRESS MULLIGRUB

Why so? Why, did not you send the self-same fellow for the jole of salmon that had the cup?

MULLIGRUB

'Tis well,—'tis very well.

MISTRESS MULLIGRUB

And will'd me to come and eat it with you at the goldsmith's?

MULLIGRUB

O, ay, ay, ay,—art in thy right wits?

MISTRESS MULLIGRUB

Do you hear?—make a fool of somebody else; and you make an ass of me, I'll make an ox of you,—do ye see?

MULLIGRUB

Nay, wife, be patient; for, look you, I may be mad, or drunk, or so; for my own part, though you can bear more than I, yet I can do well. I will not curse nor cry, but Heaven knows what I think. Come, let's go hear some music; I will never more say my prayers. Let's go hear some doleful music. Nay, if Heaven forget to prosper knaves, I'll go no more to the synagogue. Now I am discontented, I'll turn sectary; that is fashion.

[Exeunt.

ACT IV

SCENE I

Room in Sir Hubert Subboys' house.

Enter **SIR HUBERT SUBBOYS, SIR LIONEL FREEVILL, CRISPINELLA; SERVANTS** with lights.

SIR HUBERT
More lights! Welcome, Sir Lionel Freevill! brother Freevill, shortly. Look to your lights!

SERVANT
The masquers are at hand.

SIR LIONEL
Call down our daughter. Hark! they are at hand: rank handsomely.

[Enter the **MASQUERS**; they dance. Enter **BEATRICE**, **FREEVILL**, and **MALHEUREUX**. **MALHEUREUX** takes **BEATRICE** from **FREEVILL**: they draw.

FREEVILL
Know, sir, I have the advantage of the place;
You are not safe: I would deal even with you.

MALHEUREUX
So.

[They exchange gloves as pledges.

FREEVILL
So.

BEATRICE
I do beseech you, sweet, do not for me provoke your fortune.

SIR LIONEL
What sudden flaw is risen?

SIR HUBERT
From whence comes this?

FREEVILL
An ulcer, long time lurking, now is burst.

SIR HUBERT
Good sir, the time and your designs are soft.

BEATRICE
Ay, dear sir, counsel him, advise him; 'twill relish well
From your carving. Good my sweet, rest safe.

FREEVILL
All's well! all's well!—this shall be ended straight.

SIR HUBERT
The banquet stays;—there we'll discourse more large.

FREEVILL
Marriage must not make men cowards.

SIR LIONEL
Nor rage fools.

SIR HUBERT
'Tis valour not where heat but reason rules.

[Exeunt; only **TYSEFEW** and **CRISPINELLA** stay.

TYSEFEW
But do you hear, lady?—you proud ape, you! What was the jest you brake of me even now?

CRISPINELLA
Nothing. I only said you were all mettle;—that you had a brazen face, a leaden brain, and a copper beard.

TYSEFEW
Quicksilver,—thou little more than a dwarf, and something less than a woman.

CRISPINELLA
A wisp! a wisp! a wisp!—will you go to the banquet?

TYSEFEW
By the Lord, I think thou wilt marry shortly too; thou growest somewhat foolish already.

CRISPINELLA
O, i'faith, 'tis a fair thing to be married, and a necessary. To hear this word must! If our husbands be proud, we must bear his contempt; if noisome, we must bear with the goat under his armholes; if a fool, we must bear his bable; and, which is worse, if a loose liver, we must live upon unwholesome reversions; where, on the contrary side, our husbands—because they may, and we must—care not for us. Things hoped with fear, and got with strugglings, are men's high pleasures, when duty palls and flats their appetite.

TYSEFEW
What a tart monkey is this! By heaven! if thou hadst not so much wit, I could find in my heart to marry thee. Faith, bear with me for all this!

CRISPINELLA
Bear with thee? I wonder how thy mother could bear thee ten months in her belly, when I cannot endure thee two hours in mine eye.

TYSEFEW
Alas, for your sweet soul! By the Lord, you are grown a proud, scurvy, apish, idle, disdainful, scoffing—God's foot! because you have read Euphues and his England, Palmerin de Oliva, and the Legend of Lies!

CRISPINELLA

Why, i'faith, yet, servant, you of all others should bear with my known unmalicious humours: I have always in my heart given you your due respect. And Heaven may be sworn, I have privately given fair speech of you, and protested—

TYSEFEW

Nay, look you; for my own part, if I have not as religiously vow'd my heart to you,—been drunk to your health, swallowed flap-dragons, ate glasses, drunk urine, stabb'd arms, and done all the offices of protested gallantry for your sake; and yet you tell me I have a brazen face, a leaden brain, and a copper beard! Come, yet, and it please you.

CRISPINELLA

No, no;—you do not love me.

TYSEFEW

By—but I do now; and whosoever dares say that I do not love you, nay, honour you, and if you would vouchsafe to marry—

CRISPINELLA

Nay, as for that, think on't as you will, but God's my record,—and my sister knows I have taken drink and slept upon't,—that if ever I marry, it shall be you; and I will marry, and yet I hope I do not say it shall be you neither.

TYSEFEW

By Heaven, I shall be as soon weary of health as of your enjoying!—Will you cast a smooth cheek upon me?

CRISPINELLA

I cannot tell. I have no crump'd shoulders, my back needs no mantle, and yet marriage is honourable. Do you think ye shall prove a cuckold?

TYSEFEW

No, by the Lord, not I!

CRISPINELLA

Why, I thank you, i'faith. Heigho! I slept on my back this morning, and dreamt the strangest dreams. Good Lord! How things will come to pass! Will you go to the banquet?

TYSEFEW

If you will be mine, you shall be your own:—my purse, my body, my heart, is yours,—only be silent in my house, modest at my table, and wanton in my bed;—and the Empress of Europe cannot content, and shall not be contented, better.

CRISPINELLA

Can any kind heart speak more discreetly affectionately? My father's consent; and as for mine—

TYSEFEW

Then thus, and thus, so Hymen should begin; Sometimes a falling out proves falling in.

[Exeunt.

Near Sir Hubert Subboys' house.

Enter **FREEVILL**, speaking to some within; **MALHEUREUX** at the other door.

FREEVILL
As you respect my virtue, give me leave
To satisfy my reason, though not blood.—
So all runs right; our feignèd rage hath ta'en
To fullest life: they are much possess'd
Of force most, most all quarrel. Now, my right friend,
Resolve me with open breast, free and true heart;
Cannot thy virtue, having space to think
And fortify her weakened powers with reason,
Discourses, meditations, discipline,
Divine ejaculatories, and all those aids against devils,—
Cannot all these curb thy low appetite
And sensual fury?

MALHEUREUX
There is no God in blood, no reason in desire.
Shall I but live? Shall I not be forced to act
Some deed whose very name is hideous?

FREEVILL
No.

MALHEUREUX
Then I must enjoy Franceschina.

FREEVILL
You shall.
I'll lend this ring: show it to that fair devil:
It will resolve me dead;
Which rumour, with my artificial absence,
Will make most firm: enjoy her suddenly.

MALHEUREUX
But if report go strong that you are slain,
And that by me,—whereon I may be seized,—
Where shall I find your being?

FREEVILL
At Master Shatewe's the jeweller's, to whose breast
I'll trust our secret purpose.

MALHEUREUX
Ay, rest yourself;
Each man hath follies.

FREEVILL
But those worst of all,
Who, with a willing eye, do seeing fall.

MALHEUREUX
'Tis true, but truth seems folly in madness' spectacles. I am not now myself, no man: farewell.

FREEVILL
Farewell.

MALHEUREUX
When woman's in the heart, in the soul hell.

[Exit **MALHEUREUX**.

FREEVILL
Now, repentance, the fool's whip, seize thee;
Nay, if there be no means I'll be thy friend,
But not thy vices'; and with greatest sense
I'll force thee feel thy errors to the worst;
The wildest of dangers thou shalt sink into.
No jeweller shall see me; I will lurk
Where none shall know or think; close I'll withdraw,
And leave thee with two friends—a whore and knave;
But is this virtue in me? No, not pure,
Nothing extremely best with us endures;
No use in simple purities; the elements
Are mix'd for use; silver without allay
Is all too eager to be wrought for use:
Nor precise virtues, ever purely good,
Holds useful size with temper of weak blood.
Then let my course be borne, though with side-wind;
The end being good, the means are well assign'd.

[Exit.

Franceschina's lodging.

Enter **FRANCESCHINA** melancholy, **COCLEDEMOY** leading her.

COCLEDEMOY
Come, catafugo, Frank o' Frank-hall! who, who ho! Excellent! Ha, here's a plump-rump'd wench, with a breast softer than a courtier's tongue, an old lady's gums, or an old man's mentula. My fine rogue—

FRANCESCHINA
Pah, you poltroon!

COCLEDEMOY
Goody fist, flumpum pumpum; ah, my fine wag-tail, thou art as false, as prostituted, and adulterate as some translated manuscript. Buss, fair whore, buss!

FRANCESCHINA
God's sacrament, pox!

COCLEDEMOY
Hadamoy key, dost thou frown, medianthon teukey? Nay, look here. Numeron key, silver blithefor cany, os cany goblet: us key ne moy blegefoy oteeston pox, on you gosling!

FRANCESCHINA
By me fait, dis bin very fine langage; ick sall bush ye now; ha, be garzon, vare had you dat plate?

COCLEDEMOY
Hedemoy key, get you gone, punk rampant, key, common up-tail!

[Enter **MARY FAUGH** in haste.

MARY FAUGH
O daughter, cousin, niece, servant, mistress!

COCLEDEMOY
Humpum, plumpum squat, I am gone.

[Exit **COCLEDEMOY**.

MARY FAUGH
There is one Master Malheureux at the door desires to see you. He says he must not be denied, for he hath sent this ring; and withal says 'tis done.

FRANCESCHINA
Vat sall me do now, God's sacrament! Tell him two hours hence he sall be most affectionately velcome; tell him (vat sall me do?), tel him ick am bin in my bate, and ick sall perfume my feets, mak a mine body so delicate for his arm, two hours hence.

MARY FAUGH

I shall satisfy him: two hours hence, well.

[Exit **MARY FAUGH**.

FRANCESCHINA
Now ick sall revange; hay, begar, me sal tartar de whole generation! Mine brain vork it. Freevill is dead, Malheureux sall hang; and mine rival, Beatrice, ick sall make run mad.

[Enter **MARY FAUGH**.

MARY FAUGH
He's gone, forsooth, to eat a caudle of cock-stones, and will return within this two hours.

FRANCESCHINA
Verie vel, give monies to some fellow to squire me; ick sal go abroad.

MARY FAUGH
There's a lusty bravo beneath, a stranger, but a good stale rascal. He swears valiantly, kicks a bawd right virtuously, and protests with an empty pocket right desperately. He'll squire you.

FRANCESCHINA
Very velcom; mine fan; ick sall retorn presantly. Now sal me be revange; ten tousant devla! der sall be no got in me but passion, no tought but rage, no mercy but bloud, no spirit but divla in me. Dere sal noting tought good for me, but dat is mischievous for others.

[Exit.

SCENE IV

Room in Sir Hubert Subboys' house.

Enter **SIR HUBERT**, **SIR LIONEL**, **BEATRICE**, **CRISPINELLA**, and **NURSE**, **TYSEFEW** following.

SIR LIONEL
Did no one see him since?—pray God!—nay, all is well.
A little heat; what? he is but withdrawn;
And yet I would to God!—but fear you nothing.

BEATRICE
Pray God that all be well, or would I were not!

TYSEFEW
He's not to be found, sir, anywhere.

SIR LIONEL

You must not make a heavy face presage an ill event. I like your sister well, she's quick and lively: would she would marry, faith.

CRISPINELLA
Marry, nay and I would marry, methinks an old man's a quiet thing.

SIR LIONEL
Ha, mass! and so he is.

CRISPINELLA
You are a widower?

SIR LIONEL
That I am, i'faith, fair Crisp; and I can tell you, would you affect me, I have it in me yet, i'faith.

CRISPINELLA
Troth I am in love; let me see your hand: would you cast yourself away upon me willingly?

SIR LIONEL
Will I? Ay, by the—

CRISPINELLA
Would you be a cuckold willingly? By my troth 'tis a comely, fine, and handsome sight, for one of my years to marry an old man; truth, 'tis restorative; what a comfortable thing it is to think of her husband, to hear his venerable cough o' the everlastings, to feel his rough skin, his summer hands and winter legs, his almost no eyes, and assuredly no teeth; and then to think what she must dream of, when she considers others' happiness and her own want! 'tis a worthy and notorious comfortable match.

SIR LIONEL
Pish, pish! will you have me?

CRISPINELLA
Will you assure me—

SIR LIONEL
Five hundred pound jointure?

CRISPINELLA
That you will die within this fortnight?

SIR LIONEL
No, by my faith, **CRISPINELLA**

CRISPINELLA
Then Crisp by her faith assures you she'll have none of you.

[Enter **YOUNG FREEVILL** disguised like a pander, and **FRANCESCHINA**.

FREEVILL
By'r leave, gentles and men of nightcaps, I would speak, but that here stands one is able to express her own tale best.

FRANCESCHINA
Sir, mine speech is to you; you had a son, matre Freevill?

SIR LIONEL
Had, ha! and have.

FRANCESCHINA
No point, me am come to assure you dat one mestre Malheureux hath killed him.

BEATRICE
O me! wretched, wretched!

SIR HUBERT
Look to our daughter.

SIR LIONEL
How art thou inform'd?

FRANCESCHINA
If dat it please you to go vid me, ick sall bring you where you sall hear Malheureux vid his own lips confess it, and dare ye may apprehend him, and revenge your and mine love's blood.

SIR HUBERT
Your love's blood! mistress, was he your love?

FRANCESCHINA
He was so, sir; let your daughter hear it: do not veep, lady; de young man dat be slain did not love you, for he still lovit me ten tousant tousant times more dearly.

BEATRICE
O my heart, I will love you the better; I cannot hate what he affected. O passion, O my grief! which way wilt break, think, and consume!

CRISPINELLA
Peace!

BEATRICE
Dear woes cannot speak.

FRANCESCHINA
For look you, lady, dis your ring he gave me, vid most bitter jests at your scorn'd kindness.

BEATRICE

He did not ill not to love me, but sure he did not well to mock me: gentle minds will pity, though they cannot love; yet peace and my love sleep with him. Unlace, good nurse; alas! I was not so ambitious of so supreme an happiness, that he should only love me; 'twas joy enough for me, poor soul, that I only might only love him.

FRANCESCHINA
O but to be abused, scorn'd, scoff'd at! O ten tousand divla, by such a one, and unto such a one!

BEATRICE
I think you say not true, sister; shall we know one another in the other world?

CRISPINELLA
What means my sister?

BEATRICE
I would fain see him again! O my tortured mind!
Freevill is more than dead, he is unkind!

[Exeunt **BEATRICE**, **CRISPINELLA**, and **NURSE**.

SIR HUBERT
Convey her in, and so, sir, as you said, Set a strong watch.

SIR LIONEL
Ay, sir, and so pass along with this same common woman; you must make it good.

FRANCESCHINA
Ick sall, or let me pay for his mine bloud.

SIR HUBERT
Come, then, along all, with quiet speed.

SIR LIONEL
O fate!

TYSEFEW
O sir, be wisely sorry, but not passionate.

[Exeunt all but **YOUNG FREEVILL**.

FREEVILL
I will go and reveal myself! stay, no, no;
Grief endears love. Heaven! to have such a wife
Is happiness to breed pale envy in the saints.
Thou worthy dove-like virgin without gall,
Cannot (that woman's evil) jealousy,
Despite disgrace, nay, which is worse, contempt,
Once stir thy faith? O truth, how few sisters hast thou!

Dear memory!
With what a suffering sweetness, quiet modesty,
Yet deep affection, she received my death!
And then with what a patient, yet oppressed kindness,
She took my lewdly intimated wrongs!
O the dearest of heaven! were there but three
Such women in the world, two might be saved.
Well, I am great
With expectation to what devilish end
This woman of foul soul will drive her plots;
But Providence all wicked art o'ertops;
And impudence must know (tho' stiff as ice),
That fortune doth not always dote on vice.

[Exit.

SCENE V

A Street.

Enter **SIR HUBERT**, **SIR LIONEL**, **TYSEFEW**, **FRANCESCHINA**, and **THREE** with halberds.

SIR HUBERT
Plant a watch there! be very careful, sirs; the rest with us.

TYSEFEW
The heavy night grows to her depth of quiet;

'Tis about mid-darkness.

FRANCESCHINA
Mine shambre is hard by; ick sall bring you to it presantment.

SIR LIONEL
Deep silence! On!

[Exeunt.

COCLEDEMOY [Within]
Wa, ha, ho!

[Enter **MULLIGRUB**.

MULLIGRUB

It was his voice, 'tis he: he sups with his cupping-glasses. 'Tis late; he must pass this way: I'll ha' him—I'll ha' my fine boy, my worshipful Cocledemoy; I'll moy him; he shall be hang'd in lousy linen; I'll hire some sectary to make him an heretic before he die; and when he is dead I'll piss on his grave.

[Enter **COCLEDEMOY**.

COCLEDEMOY
Ah, my fine punks, good night, Frank Frailty, Frail o' Frail-hall! Bonus noches, my ubiquitari.

MULLIGRUB
Ware polling and shaving, sir.

COCLEDEMOY
A wolf, a wolf, a wolf!

[Exit **COCLEDEMOY**, leaving his cloak behind him.

MULLIGRUB
Here's something yet, a cloak, a cloak! Yet I'll after; he cannot 'scape the watch; I'll hang him if I have any mercy. I'll slice him.

[Exit.

[Enter **THREE CONSTABLES**; to them **COCLEDEMOY**.

1ST CONSTABLE
Who goes there? Come before the constable.

COCLEDEMOY
Bread o' God! constable, you are a watch for the devil. Honest men are robb'd under your nose; there's a false knave in the habit of a vintner set upon me; he would have had my purse, but I took me to my heels: yet he got my cloak, a plain stuff cloak, poor, yet 'twill serve to hang him. 'Tis my loss, poor man that I am!

[Exit.

[Enter **MULLIGRUB** running with Cocledemoy's cloak.

2ND CONSTABLE
Masters, we must watch better; is't not strange that knaves, drunkards, and thieves should be abroad, and yet we of the watch, scriveners, smiths, and tailors, never stir?

1ST CONSTABLE
Hark, who goes there?

MULLIGRUB
An honest man and a citizen.

2ND CONSTABLE
Appear, appear; what are you?

MULLIGRUB
A simple vintner.

1ST CONSTABLE
A vintner ha! and simple; draw nearer, nearer; here's the cloak.

2ND CONSTABLE
Ay, Master Vintner, we know you: a plain stuff cloak; 'tis it.

1ST CONSTABLE
Right, come! O thou varlet, dost not thou know that the wicked cannot 'scape the eyes of the constable?

MULLIGRUB
What means this violence? As I am an honest man I took the cloak—

1ST CONSTABLE
As you are a knave, you took the cloak, we are your witnesses for that.

MULLIGRUB
But, hear me, hear me! I'll tell you what I am.

2ND CONSTABLE
A thief you are.

MULLIGRUB
I tell you my name is Mulligrub.

1ST CONSTABLE
I will grub you. In with him to the stocks; there let him sit till to-morrow morning, that Justice Quodlibet may examine him.

MULLIGRUB
Why, but I tell thee—

2ND CONSTABLE
Why, but I tell thee, we'll tell thee now.

MULLIGRUB
Am I not mad? am I not an ass? Why, scabs, God's-foot! let me out.

2ND CONSTABLE
Ay, ay, let him prate; he shall find matter in us scabs, I warrant: God's-so, what good members of the commonwealth do we prove!

1ST CONSTABLE

Prithee, peace; let's remember our duties, and let's go sleep, in the fear of God.

[Exeunt, having left **MULLIGRUB** in the stocks.

MULLIGRUB
Who goes there? Illo, ho, ho: zounds, shall I run mad—lose my wits! Shall I be hang'd? Hark; who goes there? Do not fear to be poor, Mulligrub; thou hast a sure stock now.

[Re-enter **COCLEDEMOY** like a bellman.

COCLEDEMOY
The night grows old,
And many a cuckold
Is now—Wha, ha, ha, ho!
Maids on their backs
Dream of sweet smacks,
And warm—Wo, ho, ho, ho!
I must go comfort my venerable Mulligrub, I must fiddle him till he fist. Fough!
Maids in your night-rails,
Look well to your light—
Keep close your locks,
And down your smocks;
Keep a broad eye,
And a close thigh.
Excellent, excellent! Who's there? Now, Lord, Lord—Master Mulligrub—deliver us! what does your worship in the stocks? I pray come out, sir.

MULLIGRUB
Zounds, man, I tell thee I am lock'd!

COCLEDEMOY
Lock'd! O world! O men! O time! O night! that canst not discern virtue and wisdom, and one of the common council! What is your worship in for?

MULLIGRUB
For (a plague on't) suspicion of felony.

COCLEDEMOY
Nay, and it be such a trifle, Lord, I could weep, to see your good worship in this taking. Your worship has been a good friend to me, and tho' you have forgot me, yet I knew your wife before she was married, and since I have found your worship's door open, and I have knock'd, and God knows what I have saved: and do I live to see your worship stocked?

MULLIGRUB
Honest bellman, I perceive
Thou knowest me: I prithee call the watch.
Inform the constable of my reputation,
That I may no longer abide in this shameful habitation,

And hold thee all I have about me.

[Gives him his purse.

COCLEDEMOY
'Tis more than I deserve, sir: let me alone for your delivery.

MULLIGRUB
Do, and then let me alone with Cocledemoy. I'll moy him!

[Re-enter the **CONSTABLES**.

COCLEDEMOY
Maids in your—
Master Constable, whose that ith' stocks?

1ST CONSTABLE
One for a robbery: one Mulligrub, he calls himself. Mulligrub? Bellman, knowest thou him?

COCLEDEMOY
Know him! O, Master Constable, what good service have you done! Know him? He's a strong thief; his house has been suspected for a bawdy tavern a great while, and a receipt for cut-purses, 'tis most certain. He has been long in the black book, and is he ta'en now?

2ND CONSTABLE
By'r lady, my masters, we'll not trust the stocks with him, we'll have him to the justices, get a mittimus to Newgate presently. Come, sir, come on, sir.

MULLIGRUB
Ha! does your rascalship yet know my worship in the end?

1ST CONSTABLE
Ay, the end of your worship we know.

MULLIGRUB
Ha! goodman constable, here's an honest fellow can tell you what I am?

2ND CONSTABLE
'Tis true, sir; y'are a strong thief, he says, on his own knowledge. Bind fast, bind fast! we know you. We'll trust no stocks with you. Away with him to the jail instantly.

MULLIGRUB
Why, but dost hear? Bellman, rogue, rascal! God's—why, but—

[The **CONSTABLES** drag away **MULLIGRUB**.

COCLEDEMOY

Why, but! wha, ha, ha! excellent, excellent! ha, my fine Cocledemoy, my vintner fists. I'll make him fart crackers before I ha' done with him; to-morrow is the day of judgment. Afore the Lord God, my knavery grows unperegall; 'tis time to take a nap, until half an hour hence. God give your worship music, content, and rest.

[Exit.

SCENE I

Franceschina's lodging.

Enter **FRANCESCHINA**, **SIR LIONEL**, **TYSEFEW**, with **OFFICERS**.

FRANCESCHINA
You bin very velcom to mine shambra.

SIR LIONEL
But, how know ye, how are ye assured,
Both of the deed, and of his sure return?

FRANCESCHINA
O min-here, ick sall tell you. Metre Malheureux came all bretless running a my shambra, his sword all bloudy: he tel a me he had kil Freevill, and pred a me to conceal him. Ick flatter him, bid bring monies, he should live and lie vid me. He went, whilst ick (me hope vidout sins), out of mine mush love to Freevill, betray him.

SIR LIONEL
Fear not, 'tis well: good works get grace for sin.

[She conceals them behind the curtain.

FRANCESCHINA
Dere, peace, rest dere; so, softly, all go in.—
De net is lay, now sal ick be revenge.
If dat me knew a dog dat Freevill love,
Me would puisson him; for know de deepest hell
As a revenging woman's naught so fell.

[Enter **MARY FAUGH**.

MARY FAUGH
Ho! Cousin Frank, the party you wot of, Master Malheureux—

FRANCESCHINA

Bid him come up, I prede.

[Cantat saltatque cum cithara.

[Enter **MALHEUREUX**.

FRANCESCHINA
O min-here man, a dere liver love,
Mine ten tousant times velcom love!
Ha! by mine trat, you bin de just—vat sall me say?
Vat seet honie name sall I call you?

MALHEUREUX
Any from you
Is pleasure. Come, my loving prettiness,
Where's thy chamber? I long to touch your sheets.

FRANCESCHINA
No, no, not yet, mine seetest soft-lipp'd love,
You sall not gulp down all delights at once.
Be min trat, dis all-fles-lovers, dis ravenous wenchers dat sallow all down hole, vill have all at one bit; fie,
fie, fie! be min fait, dey do eat comfets vid spoons.
No, no, I'll make you chew your pleasure vit love;
De more degrees and steps, de more delight,
De more endearèd is de pleasure height.

MALHEUREUX
What, you're a learn'd wanton, and proceed by art?

FRANCESCHINA
Go, little vag, pleasure should have a crane's long neck, to relish de ambrosia of delight. And ick pre de
tell me, for me loves to hear of manhood very mush, i'fait: ick prede—vat vas me a saying? Oh, ick prede
tell a me how did you killa Metre Freevill?

MALHEUREUX
Why, quarrelled o' set purpose, drew him out,
Singled him, and, having the advantage
Of my sword and might, ran him through and through.

FRANCESCHINA
Vat did you vid him van he was sticken?

MALHEUREUX
I dragg'd him by the heels to the next wharf,
And spurn'd him in the river.

[Those in ambush rusheth forth and take him.

SIR LIONEL
Seize, seize him!
O monstrous! O ruthless villain!

MALHEUREUX
What mean you, gentlemen? By heaven—

TYSEFEW
Speak not of anything that's good.

MALHEUREUX
Your errors gives you passion: Freevill lives.

SIR LIONEL
Thy own lips say thou liest.

MALHEUREUX
Let me die, if at Shatewe's the jeweller he lives not safe untouch'd.

TYSEFEW
Meantime to strictest guard, to sharpest prison.

MALHEUREUX
No rudeness, gentlemen: I'll go undragg'd.
O, wicked, wicked devil!

[Exit.

SIR LIONEL
Sir, the day of trial is this morn; let's prosecute
The sharpest rigour and severest end:
Good men are cruel when they're vice's friend.

SIR HUBERT
Woman, we thank thee with no empty hand;
Strumpets are fit for something. Farewell.

[ALL save YOUNG FREEVILL depart.

FREEVILL
Ay, for hell!
O, thou unreprievable, beyond all
Measure of grace damn'd irremediably!
That things of beauty created for sweet use,
Soft comfort, as the very music of life,
Custom should make so unutterably hellish!
O, heaven!
What difference is in women and their life!

What man, but worthy name of man, would leave
The modest pleasures of a lawful bed—
The holy union of two equal hearts
Mutually holding either dear as health—
Th' undoubted issues, joys of chaste sheets,
Th' unfeign'd embrace of sober ignorance—
To twine th' unhealthful loins of common loves,
The prostituted impudence of things,
Senseless like those by cataracts of Nile,
Their use so vile takes away sense! How vile
To love a creature made of blood and hell,
Whose use makes weak, whose company doth shame,
Whose bed doth beggar, issue doth defame!

[Re-enter **FRANCESCHINA**.

FRANCESCHINA
Metre Freevill live? ha, ha, live at Mestre Shatewe's! Mush at Metre Shatewe's! Freevill is dead,
Malheureux sall hang: and, sweet divel, dat Beatrice would but run mad, dat she would but run mad!
den me would dance and sing. Metre Don Dubon, me pre ye now go to Mestres Beatrice. Tell her
Freevill is sure dead, and dat he curse herself especially, for dat he was sticked in her quarrel, swearing
in his last gasp, dat if it had bin in mine quarrels 'twould never have grieved him.

FREEVILL
I will.

FRANCESCHINA
Prede do, and say any ting dat vil vex her.

FREEVILL
Let me alone to vex her.

FRANCESCHINA
Vil you, vil you mak a her run mad? Here, take dis ring, see me scorn to wear anyting dat was hers or his.
I prede torment her, ick cannot love her; she honest and virtuous, forsooth!

FREEVILL
Is she so? O vile creature! then let me alone with her.

FRANCESCHINA
Vat, vil you mak a her mad? seet, by min trat, be pretta servan; bush, ick sall go to bet now.

[Exit.

FREEVILL
Mischief, whither wilt thou? O thou tearless woman!
How monstrous is thy devil,
The end of hell as thee!

How miserable were it to be virtuous,
If thou couldst prosper!
I'll to my love, the faithful Beatrice;
She has wept enough, and faith, dear soul, too much.
But yet how sweet is it to think how dear
One's life was to his love: how mourn'd his death!
'Tis joy not to be express'd with breath:
But O let him that would such passion drink,
Be quiet of his speech, and only think!

[Exit.

SCENE II

Beatrice's chamber.

Enter Beatrice and Crispinella.

BEATRICE
Sister, cannot a woman kill herself? is it not lawful to die when we should not live?

CRISPINELLA
O sister, 'tis a question not for us; we must do what God will.

BEATRICE
What God will? Alas, can torment be His glory, or our grief His pleasure! Does not the nurse's nipple, juiced over with wormwood, bid the child it should not suck? And does not Heaven, when it hath made our breath bitter unto us, say we should not live?
O my best sister,
To suffer wounds when one may 'scape this rod
Is against nature, that is against God!

CRISPINELLA
Good sister,
Do not make me weep; sure Freevill was not false.
I'll gage my life that strumpet, out of craft
And some close second end, hath maliced him.

BEATRICE
O sister! if he were not false, whom have I lost?
If he were, what grief to such unkindness!
From head to foot I am all misery;
Only in this, some justice I have found—
My grief is like my love, beyond all bound.

[Enter **NURSE**.

NURSE
My servant, Master Caqueteur, desires to visit you.

CRISPINELLA
For grief's sake keep him out; his discourse is like the long word Honorificabilitudinitatibus, a great deal of sound and no sense: his company is like a parenthesis to a discourse,—you may admit it, or leave it out, it makes no matter.

[Enter **FREEVILL** in his disguise.

FREEVILL
By your leave, sweet creatures.

CRISPINELLA
Sir, all I can yet say of you is, you are uncivil.

FREEVILL
You must deny it. By your sorrow's leave,
I bring some music to make sweet your grief.

BEATRICE
Whate'er you please. O break my heart!
Canst thou yet pant? O dost thou yet survive?
Thou didst not love him if thou now canst live!

[**FREEVILL** sings.
O Love, how strangely sweet
Are thy weak passions!
That love and joy should meet
In self-same fashions!
O who can tell
The cause why this should move?
But only this,—
No reason ask of Love!

[**BEATRICE** swounds.

CRISPINELLA
Hold, peace!—the gentlest soul is sownd. O my best sister!

FREEVILL
Ha, get you gone, close the doors! My Beatrice!

[Discovers himself.

Cursed be my indiscreet trials! O my immeasurably loving—

CRISPINELLA

She stirs, give air, she breathes!

BEATRICE

Where am I? Ha! how have I slipp'd off life?
Am I in heaven? O my lord, though not loving,
By our eternal being, yet give me leave
To rest by thy dear side! Am I not in heaven?

FREEVILL

O eternally much loved, recollect your spirits!

BEATRICE

Ha, you do speak! I do see you, I do live!
I would not die now: let me not burst with wonder.

FREEVILL

Call up your blood; I live to honour you
As the admired glory of your sex.
Nor ever hath my love been false to you;
Only I presum'd to try your faith too much,
For which I most am grieved.

CRISPINELLA

Brother, I must be plain with you, you have wrong'd us.

FREEVILL

I am not so covetous to deny it;
But yet, when my discourse hath stay'd your quaking,
You will be smoother lipp'd; and the delight
And satisfaction which we all have got,
Under these strange disguisings, when you know,
You will be mild and quiet, forget at last:
It is much joy to think on sorrows past.

BEATRICE

Do you then live? and are you not untrue?
Let me not die with joy; pleasure's more extreme
Than grief; there's nothing sweet to man but mean.

FREEVILL

Heaven cannot be too gracious to such goodness.
I shall discourse to you the several chances;
But hark, I must yet rest disguis'd;
The sudden close of many drifts now meet:
Where pleasure hath some profit, art is sweet.

[Enter **TYSEFEW**.

TYSEFEW
News, news, news, news!

CRISPINELLA
Oysters, oysters, oysters, oysters!

TYSEFEW
Why, is not this well now? Is not this better than louring and pouting and puling, which is hateful to the living and vain to the dead? Come, come, you must live by the quick, when all is done; and for my own part, let my wife laugh at me when I am dead, so she'll smile upon me whilst I live: but to see a woman whine, and yet keep her eyes dry: mourn, and yet keep her cheeks fat: nay, to see a woman claw her husband by the feet when he is dead, that would have scratched him by the face when he was living—this now is somewhat ridiculous.

CRISPINELLA
Lord, how you prate.

TYSEFEW
And yet I was afraid, i'faith, that I should ha' seen a garland on this beauty's hearse; but time, truth, experience, and variety, are great doers with women.

CRISPINELLA
But what's the news?—the news, I pray you?

TYSEFEW
I pray you? ne'er pray me: for by your leave you may command me. This 'tis:
The public sessions, which this day is past,
Hath doom'd to death ill-fortuned Malheureux.

CRISPINELLA
But, sir, we heard he offer'd to make good,
That Freevill lived at Shatewe's the jeweller's—

BEATRICE
And that 'twas but a plot betwixt them two.

TYSEFEW
O, ay, ay, he gaged his life with it; but know,
When all approach'd the test, Shatewe denied
He saw or heard of any such complot,
Or of Freevill; so that his own defence
Appeared so false, that, like a madman's sword,
He stroke his own heart; he hath the course of law,
And instantly must suffer. But the jest
(If hanging be a jest, as many make it)
Is to take notice of one Mulligrub,
A sharking vintner.

FREEVILL
What of him, sir?

TYSEFEW
Nothing but hanging: the whoreson slave is mad before he hath lost his senses.

FREEVILL
Was his fact clear and made apparent, sir?

TYSEFEW
No, faith, suspicious; for 'twas thus protested:
A cloak was stol'n; that cloak he had; he had it,
Himself confess'd, by force; the rest of his defence
The choler of a justice wronged in wine,
Join'd with malignance of some hasty jurors,
Whose wit was lighted by the justice' nose;
The knave was cast.
But, Lord, to hear his moan, his prayers, his wishes,
His zeal ill-timèd, and his words unpitied,
Would make a dead man rise and smile,
Whilst he observed how fear can make men vile.

CRISPINELLA
Shall we go meet the execution?

BEATRICE
I shall be ruled by you.

TYSEFEW
By my troth, a rare motion; you must haste,
For malefactors goes like the world, upon wheels.

BEATRICE [To **FREEVILL**]
Will you man us? You shall be our guide.

FREEVILL
I am your servant.

TYSEFEW
Ha, servant? Zounds, I am no companion for panders! you're best make him your love.

BEATRICE
So will I, sir; we must live by the quick, you say.

TYSEFEW
'Sdeath o' virtue! what a damn'd thing's this!
Who'll trust fair faces, tears, and vows? 'Sdeath! not I.

She is a woman,—that is,—she can lie.

CRISPINELLA
Come, come, turn not a man of time, to make all ill
Whose goodness you conceive not, since the worst of chance
Is to crave grace for heedless ignorance.

[Exeunt.

SCENE III

A Public Place.

[Enter **COCLEDEMOY**, like a sergeant.

COCLEDEMOY
So, I ha' lost my sergeant in an ecliptic mist, drunk! horrible drunk! he is fine. So now will I fit myself; I hope this habit will do me no harm; I am an honest man already. Fit, fit, fit, as a punk's tail, that serves everybody. By this time my vintner thinks of nothing but hell and sulphur; he farts fire and brimstone already. Hang toasts! the execution approacheth.

[Enter **SIR LIONEL**, **SIR HUBERT**; **MALHEUREUX**, pinioned; **TYSEFEW, BEATRICE, FREEVILL, CRISPINELLA, FRANCESCHINA**, and **HALBERDS**.

MALHEUREUX
I do not blush, although condemned by laws;
No kind of death is shameful but the cause,
Which I do know is none; and yet my lust
Hath made the one (although not cause) most just.
May I not be reprieved? Freevill is but mislodg'd;
Some lethargy hath seiz'd him—no, much malice;
Do not lay blood upon your souls with good intents;
Men may do ill, and law sometime repents.

[**COCLEDEMOY** picks **MALHEUREX'** pocket of his purse.

SIR LIONEL
Sir, sir, prepare; vain is all lewd defence.

MALHEUREUX
Conscience was law, but now law's conscience.
My endless peace is made; and to the poor,—
My purse, my purse!

COCLEDEMOY
Ay, sir; and it shall please you, the poor has your purse already.

MALHEUREUX

You are a wily man.

—But now, thou source of devils, oh, how I loathe
The very memory of that I adored!
He that's of fair blood, well mien'd, of good breeding,
Best famed, of sweet acquaintance, and true friends,
And would with desperate impudence lose all these,
And hazard landing at this fatal shore,—
Let him ne'er kill, nor steal, but love a whore.

FRANCESCHINA

De man does rave; tinck a got, tinck a got, and bid de flesh, de world, and the dible, farewell.

MALHEUREUX

Farewell!

FREEVILL

Farewell!

[**FREEVILL** discovers himself.

FRANCESCHINA

Vat ist you see?—Hah!

FREEVILL

Sir, your pardon, with my this defence:
Do not forget protested violence
Of your low affections: no requests,
No arguments of reason, no known danger,
No assured wicked bloodiness,
Could draw your heart from this damnation.

MALHEUREUX

Why, stay!

FRANCESCHINA

Unprosperous devil, vat sall me do now?

FREEVILL

Therefore, to force you from the truer danger,
I wrought the feignèd; suffering this fair devil
In shape of woman to make good her plot:
And, knowing that the hook was deeply fast,
I gave her line at will, till, with her own vain strivings,
See here she's tired. O thou comely damnation!
Dost think that vice is not to be withstood?
O what is woman, merely made of blood!

SIR LIONEL
You maze us all; let us not be lost in darkness!

FREEVILL
All shall be lighted; but this time and place
Forbids longer speech; only what you can think
Has been extremely ill, is only hers.

SIR LIONEL
To severest prison with her! With what heart canst live—
What eyes behold a face?

FRANCESCHINA
Ick vil not speak; torture, torture your fill,
For me am worse than hang'd; me ha' lost my will.

[Exit **FRANCESCHINA** with the **GUARD**.

SIR LIONEL
To the extremest whip and jail.

FREEVILL
Frolic, how is it, sirs?

MALHEUREUX
I am myself. How long was't ere I could
Persuade my passion to grow calm to you!
Rich sense makes good bad language, and a friend
Should weigh no action, but the action's end.
I am now worthy yours; when before
The beast of man, loose blood, distemper'd us:
He that lust rules cannot be virtuous.

[Enter **MULLIGRUB**, **MISTRESS MULLIGRUB** and **OFFICERS**.

OFFICERS
On afore there! room for the prisoners!

MULLIGRUB
I pray you do not lead me to execution through Cheapside. I owe Master Burnish, the goldsmith, money, and I fear he'll set a sergeant on my back for it.

COCLEDEMOY
Trouble not your sconce, my Christian brothers, but have an eye unto the main chance. I will warrant your shoulders; as for your neck, Plinius Secundus, or Marcus Tullius Cicero, or somebody it is, says that a threefold cord is hardly broken.

MULLIGRUB

Well, I am not the first honest man that hath been cast away; and I hope shall not be the last.

COCLEDEMOY

O, sir, have a good stomach and maws; you shall have a joyful supper.

MULLIGRUB

In troth I have no stomach to it; and it please you, take my trencher; I use to fast at nights.

MISTRESS MULLIGRUB

O husband! I little thought you should have come to think on God thus soon; nay, and you had been hang'd deservedly it would never have grieved me; I have known of many honest innocent men have been hang'd deservedly: but to be cast away for nothing!

COCLEDEMOY

Good woman, hold your peace, your prittles and your prattles, your bibbles and your babbles; for I pray you hear me in private: I am a widower, and you are almost a widow; shall I be welcome to your houses, to your tables, and your other things?

MISTRESS MULLIGRUB

I have a piece of mutton and a featherbed for you at all times; I pray make haste.

MULLIGRUB

I do here make my confession: if I owe any man anything, I do heartily forgive him; if any man owe me anything, let him pay my wife.

COCLEDEMOY

I will look to your wife's payment, I warrant you.

MULLIGRUB

And now, good yoke-fellow, leave thy poor Mulligrub.

MISTRESS MULLIGRUB

Nay, then I were unkind; i'faith I will not leave you until I have seen you hang.

COCLEDEMOY

But brother, brother, you must think of your sins and iniquities; you have been a broacher of profane vessels; you have made us drink of the juice of the whore of Babylon: for whereas good ale, perrys, bragots, cyders, and metheglins, was the true ancient British and Troyan drinks, you ha' brought in Popish wines, Spanish wines, French wines, tam Marti quam Mercurio, both muscadine and malmsey, to the subversion, staggering, and sometimes overthrow of many a good Christian. You ha' been a great jumbler; O remember the sins of your nights! for your night works ha' been unsavoury in the taste of your customers.

MULLIGRUB

I confess, I confess; and I forgive as I would be forgiven. Do you know one Cocledemoy?

COCLEDEMOY

O very well. Know him!—an honest man he is, and a comely; an upright dealer with his neighbours, and their wives speak good things of him.

MULLIGRUB
Well, wheresoe'er he is, or whatsoe'er he is, I'll take it on my death he's the cause of my hanging. I heartily forgive him, and if he would come forth he might save me; for he only knows the why and the wherefore.

COCLEDEMOY
You do, from your hearts and midrifs and entrails, forgive him then? you will not let him rot in rusty irons, procure him to be hang'd in lousy linen without a song, and after he is dead piss on his grave?

MULLIGRUB
That hard heart of mine has procured all this; but I forgive as I would be forgiven.

COCLEDEMOY [Discovering himself]
Hang toasts, my worshipful Mulligrub. Behold thy Cocledemoy, my fine vintner; my castrophomical fine boy; behold and see!

TYSEFEW
Bliss o' the blessed, who would but look for two knaves here?

COCLEDEMOY
No knave, worshipful friend, no knave; for observe, honest Cocledemoy restores whatsoever he has got, to make you know that whatsoever he has done, has been only euphoniæ gratia—for wit's sake. I acquit this vintner, as he has acquitted me; all has been done for emphasis of wit, my fine boy, my worshipful friends.

TYSEFEW
Go, you are a flatt'ring knave.

COCLEDEMOY
I am so; 'tis a good thriving trade; it comes forward better than the seven liberal sciences, or the nine cardinal virtues; which may well appear in this, you shall never have flattering knave turn courtier. And yet I have read of many courtiers that have turned flattering knaves.

SIR HUBERT
Was't even but so? why, then all's well.

MULLIGRUB
I could even weep for joy.

MISTRESS MULLIGRUB
I could weep too, but God knows for what!

TYSEFEW
Here's another tack to be given—your son and daughter.

SIR HUBERT

Is't possible? heart, ay, all my heart; will you be joined here?

TYSEFEW

Yes, faith, father; marriage and hanging are spun both in one hour.

COCLEDEMOY

Why, then, my worshipful good friends, I bid myself most heartily welcome to your merry nuptials and wanton jigga-joggies.—And now, my very fine Heliconian gallants, and you, my worshipful friends in the middle region,
If with content our hurtless mirth hath been,
Let your pleased minds at our much care be seen;
For he shall find, that slights such trivial wit,
'Tis easier to reprove than better it.
We scorn to fear, and yet we fear to swell;
We do not hope 'tis best,—'tis all, if well.

[Exeunt.

John Marston – A Short Biography

John Marston was born to John and Maria Marston née Guarsi, and baptised on October 7th, 1576 at Wardington, Oxfordshire. His father was an eminent lawyer of the Middle Temple who first practiced in London and then became the counsel to Coventry and later its steward.

Marston entered Brasenose College, Oxford in 1592 and earned his BA in 1594. By 1595, he was in London, living in the Middle Temple. His interests were in poetry and play writing, although his father's will of 1599 hopes that he would not further pursue such vanities.

His brief career in literature began with a foray into the then fashionable genres of erotic epyllion and satire; erotic plays for boy actors to be performed before educated young men and members of the inns of court.

In 1598, he published 'The Metamorphosis of Pigmalion's Image and Certaine Satyres', a book of poetry in imitation of, on the one hand, Ovid, and, on the other, the Satires of Juvenal. He also published 'The Scourge of Villanie', in 1598. (these were issued under the pseudonym "W. Kinsayder.") The satire in these books is even more savage and misanthropic than the prevailing norm for other satirists of the era. Marston's style sometimes bends to the point of unintelligibility: he believed that satire should be rough and obscure. Marston seems to have been enraged by Joseph Hall's claim to be the first satirist in English; Hall comes in for some indirect retribution later in one or more of his satires. Some see William Shakespeare's Thersites and Iago, as well as the mad speeches of King Lear as influenced by 'The Scourge of Villanie'.

Marston had, however, arrived on the literary scene as the fad for verse satire was coming under pressure from the authority's censors. Both the Archbishop of Canterbury and the Bishop of London banned 'The Scourge of Villanie' had it publicly burned, along with copies of works by other satirists, on 4th June 1599.

In September 1599, John Marston began to work for the famed Philip Henslowe as a playwright. Marston proved a good match for the private stage where boy players performed racy dramas for an audience of city gallants and young members of the Inns of Court.

'Histriomastix' has been regarded as his first play; performed by either the Children of Paul's or the students of the Middle Temple in around 1599. Its performance kicked off an episode in literary history commonly known as the 'War of the Theatres'; the literary feud between Marston, Jonson and Dekker that took place between 1599 and 1602.

Around 1600, Marston wrote 'Jack Drum's Entertainment' and 'Antonio and Mellida', and in 1601 he wrote 'Antonio's Revenge', a sequel to the latter play; all three were performed by the company at Paul's. In 1601, he contributed poems to Robert Chester's 'Love's Martyr'. For Henslowe, he may have also collaborated with Dekker, Day, and Haughton on 'Lust's Dominion'.

By 1601, he was well known in London literary circles, particularly in his role as enemy to the equally brilliant and difficult Ben Jonson. Jonson, who reported that Marston had accused him of sexual profligacy, satirized Marston as Clove in 'Every Man Out of His Humour', as Crispinus in 'Poetaster', and as Hedon in 'Cynthia's Revels'. Jonson thought Marston a false poet, a vain, careless writer who plagiarised the works of others and whose works were marked by bizarre diction and ugly neologisms. For his part, Marston used Jonson as the complacent, arrogant critic Brabant Senior in 'Jack Drum's Entertainment' and as the envious, misanthropic playwright and satirist Lampatho Doria in 'What You Will'.

'The Return from Parnassus (II)', an anonymous and satirical play performed at St. John's College, Cambridge in 1601 and 1602, characterised Marston as a poet whose writings see him 'pissing against the world'.

Jonson states that at one point their 'War' boiled over into the physical when he had beaten Marston and taken his pistol. However, the two playwrights were reconciled; Marston wrote a prefatory poem for Jonson's 'Sejanus' in 1605 and dedicated 'The Malcontent' to him.

Beyond this episode Marston's career continued to gather both strength, assets and followers. In 1603, he became a shareholder in the Children of Blackfriars company, at that time known for steadily pushing the boundaries of personal satire, violence, and lewdness on stage. He wrote and produced two plays with the company. The first was 'The Malcontent' in 1603, his most famous play. This work was originally written for the children at Blackfriars and was later taken over by the Kings' Men at the Globe, with additions by John Webster. His second play for the Blackfriars children was 'The Dutch Courtesan', a satire on lust and hypocrisy, in 1604-5.

In 1605, he worked with George Chapman and Ben Jonson on 'Eastward Ho', a satire of popular taste and the vain imaginings of wealth to be found in the colony of Virginia. Chapman and Jonson were arrested for, according to Jonson, a few clauses that offended the Scots, but Marston escaped any imprisonment. Their detainment was brief, and the charges were dropped.

He married Mary Wilkes in 1605, the daughter of the Reverend William Wilkes, one of the chaplains to King James.

In 1606, Marston seems to have had mixed fortunes with the king. At times offending and at others pleasing. In 'Parasitaster, or, The Fawn', he satirized the king specifically. However, in the summer of that year, he put on a production of 'The Dutch Courtesan' for the King of Denmark's visit, with a Latin verse on King James that was presented by hand to the king. Finally, in 1607, he wrote 'The Entertainment at Ashby', a masque for the Earl of Huntingdon.

Marston took the theatre world by surprise when he gave up writing plays in 1609 at the age of thirty-three. He sold his shares in the company of Blackfriars. His departure from the literary scene may have been because of further offence he gave to the king. The king suspended performances at Blackfriars and had Marston imprisoned.

After release he moved into his father-in-law's house to study philosophy. In 1609, he became a reader at the Bodleian library at Oxford. On 24th September he was made a deacon and then a priest on 24th December 1609. In October 1616, Marston was assigned the living of Christchurch, Hampshire.

He died (accounts vary) on either the 24th or 25th June 1634 in London and was buried in the Middle Temple Church.

Tombs at that time were often inscribed with 'Memoriae Sacrum' ('Sacred to the memory') and then the occupants name and a brief account of their achievements. According to Anthony à Wood Marston's tomb stone read 'Oblivioni Sacrum' ('Sacred to Oblivion'), which was probably composed by Marston, and both self-abasing and witty in upturning the tradition.

Marston's reputation through the centuries has varied widely, like that of most of the minor Renaissance dramatists. Both 'The Malcontent' and 'The Dutch Courtesan' remained on stage in altered forms throughout the Restoration.

After the Restoration, Marston's works were largely reduced to literary history. The general resemblance of 'The Malcontent' to 'Hamlet' and Marston's role in the 'War of the Theatres' ensured that his plays would receive some scholarly attention, but they were not performed, nor widely read.

The Romantic movement in English literature unevenly resuscitated Marston's reputation. In his lectures, William Hazlitt praised Marston's genius for satire; however, if the romantic critics were willing to grant Marston's best work a place among the great accomplishments of the age, they remained aware of his inconsistency, what Swinburne would later call his 'uneven and irregular demesne'.

In the twentieth century, however, a few critics were willing to consider Marston as a writer who was very much in control of the world he created. T. S. Eliot saw that this 'irregular demesne' was a part of Marston's world and that "It is ... by giving us the sense of something behind, more real than any of the personages and their action, that Marston establishes himself among the writers of genius".

Plays and production dates

Histriomastix (play), 1599
Antonio and Mellida, London, Paul's theater, 1599–1600.
Jack Drum's Entertainment, London, Paul's theater, 1599/1600.
Antonio's Revenge, London, Paul's theater, 1600.
What You Will, London, Paul's theater, 1601.
The Malcontent, London, Blackfriars Theatre, 1603–1604; Globe Theatre, 1604.
Parasitaster, or The Fawn, London, Blackfriars theater, 1604.
Eastward Ho, by Marston, George Chapman, and Ben Jonson, London, Blackfriars theater, 1604–1605.
The Dutch Courtesan, London, Blackfriars theater, 1605.
The Wonder of Women, or The Tragedy of Sophonisba, London, Blackfriars theater, 1606.
The Spectacle Presented to the Sacred Majesties of Great Britain, and Denmark as They Passed through London, London, 31 July 1606.
The Entertainment of the Dowager-Countess of Darby, Ashby-de-la-Zouch in Leicestershire, 1607.
The Insatiate Countess, by Marston and William Barksted, London, Whitefriars Theatre, c 1608.

Books

The Metamorphosis of Pigmalions Image. And Certaine Satyres.
The Scourge of Villanie. Three Bookes of Satyres (1598; revised and enlarged edition, 1599)
Jacke Drums Entertainment: Or, The Comedie of Pasquill and Katherine (1601)
Loves Martyr: or, Rosalins Complaint, by Marston, Ben Jonson, William Shakespeare, and George Chapman (1601)
The History of Antonio and Mellida (1602)
Antonios Revenge (1602)
The Malcontent (1604)
Eastward Hoe, by Marston, Chapman, and Jonson (1605)
The Dutch Courtezan (1605)
Parasitaster, or The Fawne (1606)
The Wonder of Women, or The Tragedie of Sophonisba (1606)
What You Will (1607)
Histrio-mastix: Or, The Player Whipt (1610)
The Insatiate Countesse, by Marston and William Barksted (1613)
The Workes of Mr. J. Marston (1633); republished as Tragedies and Comedies (1633)
Comedies, Tragi-comedies; & Tragedies, Nonce Collection (1652)
Lust's Dominion, or The Lascivious Queen (probably the same play as The Spanish Moor's Tragedy), by Marston, Thomas Dekker, John Day, and William Haughton (1657)

www.ingramcontent.com/pod-product-compliance
Lightning Source LLC
Chambersburg PA
CBHW021938040426
42448CB00008B/1131